ADVAN

This fast-moving, ⌐
time-tested, proven strategies and tactics to
increase your sales and your income immediately.
~Brian Tracy – Author of *The*
Psychology of Selling

Carolyn's book, The Rainmaker's Quick Guide to
Lasting Sales Success *is full of real life Rainmaker
examples from worldwide experts, including myth
busters, tips and solid strategies. Whether you are
a seasoned professional or a beginner in sales, this
is relevant information you can use immediately
for your personal sales success.*
~ Lisa Sasevich, The Queen of Sales
Conversion www.LisaSasevich.com

*"There is no shortcut to lasting sales success, but
Carolyn's quick guide is the closest you'll find to
one. The strategies in this book are practical, wise,
and will lay the foundations to build your clients
for life."*
~ Andrew Sobel, bestselling author of *Power*
Questions, All for One,* and *Clients for Life

*This valuable sales self-help book provides an
easy to follow roadmap to creating and sustaining
profitable relationships with your customers.*
~ Andy Paul, Author of *Zero-Time Selling,*
Selling Power's list of Best Books for Sales
Success in 2013.

*If you're struggling with sales, this book is just
what you need. Using Carolyn's strategies, you'll*

discover how to get new clients and build great relationships -- without selling your soul.
~ Jill Konrath, author of *SNAP Selling* and *Selling to Big Companies*

The best part about this book is that the information is useful, practical and can be immediately applied. The second best part about this book is that the author has practiced everything she is preaching! If you want to improve your sales results, pick up this book. If you don't, cross your fingers that your competitor doesn't!
~Colleen Stanley, Author of *Emotional Intelligence for Sales Success,* Chief Selling Officer, Sales Leadership, Inc.

Carolyn's heart-centered approach to selling really resonates with me. We can lead, serve, and sell from our hearts with authenticity and success. Her coaching perspective both educates us and calls us to action. This book is a must read!
~ Dr. Maria Church, author of *Love-Based Leadership: Transform Your Life with Meaning and Abundance*

This is an easily readable book on sales. Using practical approaches and good old fashioned storytelling, Carolyn has found a way to demystify what is needed to be a successful rainmaker.
~Janice Mars, Sales Enablement Consultant

For any current or aspiring salesperson who desires to be a top performing Rainmaker, this book is a must have. Carolyn Coradeschi's engaging style of writing weaves stories from top sales experts into solid tips and strategies.

With one read sales professionals will be closing more deals.
~ Alice Kemper, President Sales Training Consultants, Inc.

I LOVED this book - its conversational style, the very simple and powerful truths that bust the myths about selling, and the feeling of being able to sell with ease and joy that it brings. In The Rainmaker's Quick Guide to Lasting Sales Success, *master sales coach Carolyn Coradeschi delivers all this and more!*
~ Karen A. Cappello, PCC, BCC, Mentor Coach and Trainer

The Rainmaker's Quick Guide to Lasting Sales Success offers real life stories that will lead to real life sales success. Carolyn weaves examples into each and every point so that by the end of the book the reader is energized and ready to hit the streets running. If you want to make revenue rain down for your company, internalize and practice the simple, yet fundamentally sound ideas presented in Carolyn's book.
~ Lisa D. Magnuson, Sales Strategist, Trainer, Consultant, Coach and Author, Top Line Sales, LLC

Carolyn Coradeschi delivers buckets of refreshing, practical advice on not only how rainmakers act, but how they think. *Quick tips on everything from how to prepare for a call to how to handle an objection are combined with real-world stories from Carolyn's vast experience and other industry sales pros. A must read for new and experienced* salespeople alike who want to achieve consistent sales success – and feel good doing it!

~ **Julie Hansen, author of *ACT Like a Sales Pro!***

Being so busy, it's always hard to find the time to "feed your brain" to keep yourself fresh. This book is a great tool to help anyone improve. The quick pointers and short chapters make it an easy read. Carolyn's stories are fun to read and convey great points and ideas you can use to help tweak your own process.

~ **Ginny Lemmerman, Sales Executive with Thomson Reuters**

This amazing book is full of great stories and powerful information on sales from one of the best in the business. I've worked with over 20,000 students in sales over the years and Carolyn Coradeschi stood out as a superstar sales professional even as a college student. I've followed her career since then and been proud to see her become a masterful sales professional and coach. This book will give you her best stories and wisdom to jumpstart your sales success.

~ **Dave Causer, International Development, Southwestern Company**

Carolyn Coradeschi has provided a simple but powerful outline for becoming a Rainmaker. She offers excellent examples and writes as if she was talking over coffee about ways to overcome the fear of selling and turn that into revenues. I recommend it for anyone needing a guide to growing sales.

~ **Lori Richardson, Top B2B Sales Influencer, CEO of Score More Sales, LLC**

Carolyn Coradeschi is a sales professional, and it is clear in the words she has captured in this book that she has a bias for helping others be the same. The stories, the experience, the humor and the hard hitting distinctions are what is going to make you sell more of your product or service and build your business and your bank account. As author of 'The First Sale Is Always to Yourself' I cannot agree more with Carolyn that therein lies the secret. Grab your copy today of The Rainmaker's Quick Guide to Lasting Sales Success *and invest in your career.*

~ Bernadette McLelland, Author of *The First Sale is Always to Yourself*

If you want to massively improve upon growing your business by confidently sharing the value that you offer others, then pick up The Rainmakers Quick Guide to Lasting Sales Success! *Carolyn Coradeschi provides you with simple yet extremely effective personal and professional sales tools to support you in being your best version of yourself... fostering trusting and long lasting relationships with your business partners.*

~ Dave Blomsterberg, Coach / Speaker / Recording Artist

In a world full of how-to sales books that offer prescriptive advice for the salesperson, Carolyn Coradeschi offers us all down-to-earth insider insights peppered with real-life stories. What a refreshing approach! She shows the reader how a combination of process and discipline, and yes, hard work, can be combined with common sense and, most of all, self-belief to achieve one's sales goals. I know I will pick up her book each day, and re-read chapters to give myself that boost of inspiration and insight that all of us need from time to time. I recommend you buy the book, read it, and then make it your daily selling companion.

~ Babette N. Ten Haken, Author of *Do YOU Mean Business?* Founder and President, Sales Aerobics for Engineers, LLC

Carolyn is truly a Rainmaker. Her quick guide to success is testament to her experience. Each step throughout the guide outlines winning approaches or skills to sales success. Her warm style of writing makes you feel a part of her world and her brilliant ability to be a storyteller inspires and demonstrates her sales skill. Her openness draws the reader in and gives great tips to becoming a Rainmaker. After reading this guide you will take away many practical tips but the greatest value is the way Carolyn brings honesty and integrity to the sales profession.

~ Bronwyn Bowery-Ireland, CEO - Funky.is

The Rainmaker's Quick Guide to Lasting Sales Success by Carolyn Coradeschi isn't a how-to book. Instead, it takes all our fears and dislike of change into account to help us DO something about becoming the best salesperson we can be. Even when talking about 'sales process' she includes examples of why salespeople don't follow one and assists us in figuring out how to change those things for ourselves. It's not just about how to sell, it's how to believe you can be a rainmaker and then make it happen. Read this book to change how you think and work.

~ Lynn Hidy, PCC, Sales Change Management

The Rainmaker's Quick Guide to Lasting Sales Success

Carolyn McGowan Coradeschi

THOMAS NOBLE BOOKS

Thomas Noble Books
Wilmington, DE
www.ThomasNobleBooks.com
ISBN: 978-0-9892357-2-3
Library of Congress Control Number: 2013940195
Printed in the United States of America
First Printing 2013
Cover design: www.Cyanotype.ca
Editing by Gwen Hoffnagle

Dedication

To my amazing husband, Andy, whom I've known and loved for 25 years. He has been my rock through it all.

And to my sons, Cole and Cooper, who both have brilliant futures ahead of them, filled with the gifts they possess and the choice of a life without limits.

"The first sale is always to yourself."
~ Alan Weiss

Table of Contents

Start Here for Sales Success

I'm a rainmaker. By the time you finish this quick guide, you will be too.

That's a pretty bold claim. I can just imagine you shaking your head and wondering, "Who is this person and why does she believe she can help me sell?"

I'm a sales coach. I've spent the last thirty years mastering the art of selling. I've sold everything from books to medical equipment to professional services, all over the United States and Europe.

To tell you the truth, I've been a top performing salesperson for a long time now, for my entire working career. I started training and mentoring other people in sales when I was just twenty years old.

Do you want to know the crazy thing about that?

Until I got my first sales job when I was nineteen years old, I was shy.

In fact, I was so shy that my family and friends thought I'd lost my marbles when I came home from college and informed them that I was going to spend the summer traveling out west and selling books door to door for the Southwestern Company.

Over the course of my thirty years as a top performing salesperson, I learned you don't have to be perfect, extroverted, or intimidating to succeed in sales. Top performing sales professionals, whether they are selling their own professional services or are working on commission selling for a corporation, all know a secret. They know how to make it rain money and sales whenever they want.

That's what I'm going to show you in this book.

A rainmaker is someone who can close sales deals and bring business into a company consistently. When you implement the tools and strategies I'm going to share with you in this book, you'll be able to generate sales whenever you want to, because you'll possess:

- An abundant supply of prospects
- A heart-centered yet bold selling approach which cultivates long-term positive and productive relationships with your clients
- Unparalleled listening skills which allow you to sell with the highest levels of integrity and honesty
- A simple yet powerful sales process so that you can lead your prospects easily to making a decision on your offer

Most importantly, this quick guide will eliminate any reluctance you may have about making sales. Once you know that you can sell, and sell successfully, you will transform your bank account and your life.

Your schedule is busy and you want to make more sales right away. I've distilled my best experience and sales training material into a concise guidebook that you can read quickly and start applying to your sales career immediately.

Approach this material with an open mind. Some of it may be in direct opposition to some of the 'killer' sales techniques you may have read in the past. I don't want you to kill anyone. Instead, I'll show you how to build great relationships with your clients and prospects so that they are delighted to do business with you.

Are you ready?

Let's go make it rain!

Here's to your success,

Carolyn Coradeschi

Agoura Hills, California

May, 2013

SECTION 1

Setting the Stage for Sales Success

Your first step in your journey to becoming a rainmaker is to look at why you are not selling as much as you want to now.

It all begins with what you think.

In this section, you'll smile as you read the most common selling myths and feel energized as you discover how rainmaker sales professionals think and act. You will also examine and discard any limiting beliefs you have about selling so that you can embrace more empowering beliefs which will transform both your sales performance and results.

Chapter 1
Selling is Scary... and Other Myths

"There is one quality that one must possess to win, and that is definiteness of purpose, the knowledge of what one wants and a burning desire to achieve it."

~ Napoleon Hill

My sons, Cole and Cooper, love the television show, *Myth Busters*. In case you are not familiar with this program, the hosts take commonly held beliefs and do all kinds of scientific experiments to determine if those beliefs are true or just myths. We're going to apply their approach to some of the most common beliefs about selling.

Over the years as a sales trainer and coach, I've had the opportunity to mentor many new sales professionals. In fact, I began as a sales mentor when I was just twenty years old. During my long career in sales training, I bet I've heard every sales myth in the book.

Why Should You Care About Sales Myths?

The first sale you make is always to yourself. To sell successfully, you need to believe that you can sell. If you believe in these sales myths, you will not be as effective as you can be.

That may sound too simplistic, but over the years, I've witnessed many breakthroughs occur when the person doing the selling simply shifted her mindset and cleared away the myths and beliefs which didn't support her success.

These myths and fears are universal. I've worked with clients who span the spectrum from selling multimillion-dollar capital equipment to self-employed coaches and speakers selling their own services. You are not the only one who has these doubts. Whew!

Let's clean out your mental closet together. It's okay to chuckle a bit about how silly some of these myths sound when you read them on paper. When these myths rattle around in your head during a slow month they can sound convincing, like the voice of reason or common sense. When you look at them on paper, they lose their power and may even seem a little funny.

Read this chapter with a smile and know that you can immediately stop all these myths and fears from holding you back.

Myth #1 Selling is Hard and Scary

When he was three years old, my son Cooper helped us prepare for a wine tasting party at our home. My husband makes wine and this party was about pairing different wines with food. While our guests were all well into their adult years, Cooper was the life of the party. He was very gregarious; wanting to greet everyone and make sure they had a good time, and many of our guests happily engaged him in conversation.

When the party was over and everyone had left, Cooper looked at me and asked, "When's the next party Mom? I just love meeting new people."

At Its Essence, Selling is Nothing More Than Meeting New People

Each morning I wonder who I will meet that day and how I'll be able to help them. I love selling because it gives me the opportunity to have great conversations, make real connections with people who I'd never have the opportunity to meet otherwise, and serve them in some way.

When you eliminate your stress and fear of selling by reframing it as simply meeting new people and finding ways to help them, everything shifts. You approach sales naturally, like you would make a new friend by listening and connecting.

It really can be that easy.

I recently had a sports injury which required physical therapy. At my first appointment with my physical therapist, he asked me about my work while he was stretching my muscles. When I said I was a sales coach, he said, "Wow, I need a sales coach. I have to give these sales presentations to doctors about my services and I just hate doing them."

There are abundant opportunities to meet new people and discover if you can help them. As you continue working with the material in this book, you'll discover that selling can be easy and natural for you too.

Myth #2 Selling is Slimy and I Have to be Unethical to Succeed

You know you are listening to this selling myth when you worry about ripping off your clients or feel you have to resort to bribery or underhanded techniques to win the sale. This myth comes from all those movies and television shows you've seen where the salesperson was a cad. Remember those tough-as-nails sales guys in *Glengarry Glen Ross* or *Tin Men*?

If you believe this myth, you may have bad memories of unpleasant sales encounters with slimy con artists who sold you an inferior product or a high-handed salesperson who made you feel pressured to buy.

Manipulative and deceptive black-hat sales techniques abound in some industries. We've all had the barrage of annoying tele-marketing calls during dinner. I once had a pen salesman try to sell me pens over the phone. He mispronounced my company's name several times and every time I objected to his offer for pens, he dropped his price and had the next best deal. His approach made me cringe and it also made me realize how many untrained and pushy salespeople are perpetuating the stereotype of a slimy salesperson. No wonder this myth is so common!

I learned in my first sales job that I was asking customers for their trust. They were giving me their hard earned money in exchange for books which I'd deliver to them in a few months. My personal reputation and the reputation of my company rested on my ability to be honest.

You are honest too, right?

Of course you are. As a coach, professional salesperson or entrepreneur, you realize that your business success is built on your good name in your industry. You'd never resort to underhanded sales techniques and risk your reputation.

Just stay true to your values and integrity and you'll never have to worry about being a slimy salesperson.

Myth #3 Selling Requires Lots of Talking….If I Speak More than My Prospect, She Will Buy

I recently attended a conference and mentioned I was looking for a new marketing team. After the conference I had a few people approach me to inquire about the position. They all had different styles. Some spent plenty of time asking questions about my business and making my needs the focus of the conversation.

Unfortunately, one person did not follow this proven approach. Instead, she barraged me with a ten minute speech about how great she was and all that she had accomplished. She did not even take a breath so that I could get a word in edgewise. I had to literally stop her and say, "But you haven't asked me any questions about what I need to see if we're a fit." It was as if she didn't hear me as she just kept on rattling on about herself until I tuned out.

If you approach a potential customer with a stale, canned sales script or a long dissertation about the greatness of your product or service, you won't sell very much.

The Best Approach to Selling is Active Listening not Active Talking

Contrary to what many may think, the 'gift of gab' is not a gift in sales. Top performing salespeople know how to put the brakes on any natural personal desire to dominate a conversation. They focus their attention externally toward their prospects, and away from the internal 'it's all about me' focus.

I recently closed a large contract which illustrates this point beautifully. Initially, I met with one of the company vice presidents.

In that meeting, the conversation was all about him, his vision, and his challenges. During that meeting he told me many stories concerning his company's challenges with their sales team and their attrition rate. In this meeting we didn't even discuss my services. I didn't need to tell him anything about my services because he sold himself on why we should have a second meeting with the full team of company vice presidents.

In the second meeting I got to know the other vice presidents. Each shared additional challenges, stories and their vision for their sales team. Soon, they started to ask me questions about my services. Because I had asked so many questions and listened so deeply, it was like putting together the perfect puzzle. I had all of the pieces and knew how to connect them to close a deal that everyone felt good about. Not only did I get the business, but they bought me lunch!

Listening is a powerful tool in the sales process.

Instead of thinking of selling as a process in which you chatter non-stop about the features and benefits of your service or product, think of selling as a conversation. You'll learn exactly how to have powerful sales conversations in chapter six of this book.

Myth #4 Hearing the Word 'No' Means I'm a Failure

Sandy, a coaching client of mine, is a life coach who was struggling to build her new business.

When we first met, she was just about ready to give up on her entrepreneurial dreams and go back to her day job because she could not get enough people to purchase her services.

When Sandy and I reviewed her sales process, we quickly identified the problem. She was terrified of rejection. Whenever Sandy had a sales conversation with a potential coaching client, she was so afraid of hearing the word 'No' that as soon as a prospect raised an objection, Sandy apologized for bothering her and ended the call.

Sandy believed that when a prospect said no to her coaching, she was rejecting Sandy personally. This hurt and made Sandy so uncomfortable that she gave up too soon on the prospect and stopped the sales process before the prospect even had an opportunity to say no.

When a prospect declines your offer, it doesn't mean he doesn't like you or will never do business with you in the future. Often it means that he does not yet see the value of what you've offered. Tomorrow may be a different story!

Myth #5 If I Don't Sell Something in the First Conversation, I'll Never Sell My Prospect Anything

Two of my favorite hobbies are running and volunteering so I combine them by serving as a youth track coach. When I coach my long distance runners, I have to remind them to pace themselves. If they are running a longer distance, such as the 1500 or 3000 meter races, it doesn't always matter if they are not leading at the end of the first lap.

The sales process is like a long distance race. Every once in a while you may close a sale in one selling conversation, but the majority of selling successes come from creative follow up activities which occur over time.

Sales coach Janice Mars tells a story about working in a large corporation with a group of salesmen who all worked in one big area called the Fishbowl. One day, one of her sales staff was having a meltdown in the Fishbowl. Janice sensed he was about to embarrass himself so she took him to a nearby café for a cup of coffee.

It turns out, this sales rep hated cold calling with a passion. Every time he got on the phone with a prospect, he felt intense pressure to close the sale immediately. When he didn't, he got increasingly frustrated. He was ready to quit.

Janice reminded him that he wasn't required to sell anything in his first call; his only task was to have a nice conversation, ask open-ended questions to determine values, needs, and opportunities, and then encourage the prospective client to take the next step, which was to schedule another conversation. Once he learned this he could relax and release the pressure to close a sale on the first call, this salesman became a high performer and enjoyed his work immensely.

When you can eliminate this myth, stop rushing the sale, and give yourself permission to devote time to developing a relationship with your prospects, you will hear yes much more often.

Myth #6 I'll Choke if I Hear Questions I Can't Answer

Most of my clients dread hearing questions or objections during the sales process. They worry that if questions or objections are raised it means the prospective client is just lining up reasons to say no to the offer. Some even try to talk faster so that the prospect can't get a word in edgewise.

Celebrate the Questions

In my experience, questions and objections are to be celebrated. When you hear a question, you know the prospective client is interested in what you are offering and willing to learn more. It's like a green light signaling you that you are making a good connection with this person and she is considering your offer.

We've all heard the adage that people love to buy but they hate to be sold. When they ask questions, prospects are looking for reasons to say yes. They have a problem and are trying to find out if you have the solution.

Your job is to welcome questions, listen carefully, and answer honestly. Then pause, and allow the prospect to process what you've said and respond with another question or statement. Your goal is to co-create a solution that adds value to their business.

Of course, you may hear a question that surprises you. When sales trainer Colleen Stanley started in sales, she sold athletic dancewear to school districts. She loved dance and was excited about the products she was promoting. She spent hours learning all the features of each leotard and pair of dance shoes.

When Colleen went to her first appointment, she was thrilled and excited to share everything she knew about her products. She met with a director for a group of several school districts with dance teams. The first question he asked her was, "So, who are your other customers?"

Colleen was stunned. She had no idea which other schools were using these products. She just blurted out, "Oh, I don't know." Then, she started talking more about the dancewear line she represented. Colleen was so genuine and enthusiastic about her products, the director liked her and gave her his business. Because Colleen answered the question honestly and didn't become flustered, she won her first large corporate sale.

Even if you get a question you can't answer immediately, you can still make a sale.

Myth #7 I Can't Begin until Everything is Perfect

This myth hampers the vast majority of new entrepreneurs I meet. They stress over getting the ideal logo, business card, website, or brochure. They may wait months while they struggle with their tag line or elevator speech.

This hesitation to begin also can occur in corporate sales. Some sales professionals spend weeks setting up complicated tracking systems, doing online research on potential clients, or going to networking meetings. While these strategies are all useful, if you are using them to look busy instead of engaging in sales conversations, you are in the grip of this sales myth.

Here's some great news: You don't have to wait until everything is perfect before you begin to make sales.

When I began coach training at the International Coach Academy, I didn't wait until I graduated to start selling my coaching. I loved coaching and couldn't wait to begin helping people move forward. As soon as I felt comfortable with the basic practices, I started selling and attracted paying clients.

My clients won because they got great coaching from a very passionate coach at an entry-level price. I won because I was able to gain experience at the craft of coaching with real clients. This helped build my business revenues quickly and gave me assurance that I had made a wise career decision.

Mary Ann, a woman in one of my sales coaching programs, is a new coach who already has thirty-one clients. Like me, she did not wait to begin selling her services until she graduated from the program. She was on fire and motivated to help others. She could not help sharing her love of coaching with prospective clients. Interestingly,

Mary Ann did not start her business with any previous sales experience. She used to be an anthropologist. She refused to believe the myth that she could not start coaching until someone told her she was ready.

My point is that as soon as you are skilled in your craft or have enough information about the product or service you are selling, you can begin to sell. Start today to sell what you can provide right now and resolve to grow in skill and confidence over time. The best way to win the game of sales is to begin and then refine your process as you go along.

Let's Pause Here and See How You Are Doing

Now that you've reviewed the seven myths about selling, how has your perspective changed?

Grab a piece of paper and draw a line down the middle of it, from top to bottom. On the left hand side, write the myths and fears you have about selling. Then, in the right hand column, use the information in this chapter to reframe your selling myths.

Here are a few examples to get you started:

The Rainmaker's Quick Guide

MYTH/FEAR	REFRAME
I don't want to be a pest and fear when I am following up, I'm being a nuisance	When I follow up I have a specific reason for doing so and provide valuable resources for my potential clients. This helps propel the sales process forward.
My prospect is not returning my calls or emails OR they said no to my product or service. I hate rejection.	I don't take no or rejection of my product or service personally. My pipeline is full and I have an abundance of prospects to meet with. I can still be a resource for this prospect in the future if there's a fit.
My prospect asked a question about price before we got into the presentation. Ugh, I hate answering price questions before I have an opportunity to present.	Great, a question – this is a buying signal and shows interest. I can answer it in a straight forward fashion and ask more questions to find out if my product/ service is a fit.

Chapter 2

10 Common Characteristics of Top Sales Professionals

"Of course motivation is not permanent. But then, neither is bathing; but it is something you should do on a regular basis."

~ Zig Ziglar

I'll admit it. I'm competitive and love to be the best. Whenever I started a new sales job, I wanted to quickly master the sales process in that industry. I'd determine the identity of the top performing salesperson and schedule a meeting. Each of these selling superstars was gracious and happy to help me.

In my thirty years of sales experience, I've been able to watch and learn from masters, rainmakers from a variety of industries. I discovered that top performing sales professionals, no matter which industry they were working in, possessed some common characteristics.

Embrace the following ten characteristics and you'll see your confidence increase and your sales numbers skyrocket.

#1 Manage Your Personal Energy

During the sales process, you transfer your positive energy to your prospective client. She will be able to sense if you are fully present and committed to her welfare, so it is important that you are at the top of your game: physically, emotionally, and mentally.

If you are stressed, worried, ill, tired, or multi-tasking, you simply won't be able to be fully present. When you take care of your health, get enough rest, exercise, and eat right, you'll have much more positive energy to share.

I run and work out at the gym almost every morning, not just because I love it, but because when I am fit, I have more positive energy to give to the people I connect with during my workday.

Dr. John J. Ratey, author of the book *SPARK*, discusses the link between exercise and productivity. His research revealed that aerobic exercise physically transforms the brain for peak performance. According to Dr. Ratey, getting your heart and lungs pumping can mean the difference between a calm, focused mind and a harried, inattentive self.

If I don't get my daily run or exercise I can feel my creativity wane and my focus falter. You don't have to become a runner like me, but to be a rainmaker who sells consistently and confidently, you need the glowing good health that comes from taking care of yourself. Plus, you'll feel more confident when you know you are looking your best.

You Can't Hide Your Lack of Energy or Self Care

Recently I interviewed a marketing specialist for a position in my company. I could hear his exhaustion in his voice. As much as I wanted to like him, he did not come across enthusiastically or powerfully so I could not hire him to represent my company.

When you are meeting with potential clients in person or on the phone, they can hear your energy. On those days when you have the flu or are exhausted, avoid making sales calls. Rest and recuperate, then try it again just as soon as you are feeling better.

People often comment on my positive energy level and say that it jumps across the phone line. I use my hands a lot and often stand up, even when I am speaking on the telephone, because it keeps me alert and adds energy to the conversation. Even if people can't see my hand gestures, getting my body involved in the conversation reminds me to keep things light and positive.

#2 Be Prepared

Successful salespeople can dance in the moment with their prospects, having an effortless conversation and let the prospect set the direction and the pace. However, a high performing salesperson isn't just winging it. She's carefully prepared so that she feels confident and ready to respond to anything.

In fact, if you have done your research and have solid knowledge of the prospect's business, you will stand out from your competitors. You may be surprised how many entrepreneurs and salespeople overlook this important preparatory stage and go into meetings 'cold'.

As the old saying goes, "You never have a second chance to make a good first impression." When you are prepared and have done your homework prior to your meetings, you will have greater confidence and be able to have a productive conversation with your prospect.

When you take time to prepare, your prospect will be impressed that you cared enough to learn a bit about him and that you can easily discuss your products and services, relating them to his unique needs.

So you can be prepared for your very next sales conversation, do some research before your next sales call. Find out:

- The primary messages in your prospect's website — look for information on values, mission statements, and company goals.

- How active is your prospect on social media? What sort of messages does she post about hobbies, personal interests or company activities?
- What press coverage has the individual or company garnered?
- What positive contribution does your prospect make in the community?

Now that you know a bit about your prospect, prepare your key messages about the value of your product or service.

- If you are a coach, be ready to share stories of former clients who have similar needs. Gather some testimonials and any metrics such as "78% of my clients achieve their goals in 90 days."
- If you are selling a training program or an educational event, consider how participation in your training could help your prospective client achieve both his business and personal goals.
- If you are selling for a corporation, collect examples from other corporations using your product or service and explain how their results align with your prospect's mission and goals.

This preparation before an initial meeting will ensure a smooth conversation that is uniquely tailored to your prospect.

However, preparation does not stop there. While you will do the bulk of your preparatory research before your initial encounter with your prospect, you still need to be prepared for subsequent conversations.

I use these questions before each of my sales conversations, both for in-person meetings and phone calls. In a short time, I can be focused, prepared, and confident for each encounter.

Before each call, ask yourself:

1. What is the goal of this call?

2. What do I need to find out during this call?

3. How do I move the process forward and gain a commitment?

#3 Be Resourceful

Resourcefulness is one of those uncelebrated characteristics that doesn't sound very sexy. However, the knowledge that you can handle just about anything that comes at you builds quiet confidence, which your prospects can hear in your voice.

I learned to be resourceful early on. My dad passed away when I was thirteen years old. It was a huge loss for everyone in our family and it changed the way we lived. Suddenly we all had new responsibilities as we adjusted to being a single parent family.

My ability to be resourceful continued to grow during my college years when I spent summers on the road selling books for the Southwestern

Company. At the beginning of each summer, our team went to a new city. We had to find our own lodging and learn to navigate neighborhoods to make door to door sales calls. There were no grownups taking care of any of the details for us. We figured it out as a team.

An Inventory of Resourcefulness

To develop your sense of resourcefulness, as a rainmaker sales professional, take an inventory of all the challenges you've already resolved in your life. Write them down. Review your list every Monday morning to remind yourself that you are resourceful and a skilled problem solver.

The great thing about claiming your resourcefulness is that it frees you from the need to be perfect. When you approach every challenge with a resourceful outlook, you'll delight your customers and continue to grow in confidence, plus you'll close more sales.

#4 Cherish Integrity

Integrity is paramount for sales success. When people know that you will keep your commitments, they trust you and are happy to buy from you.

If you tell a prospect that you will contact them on Tuesday, how will they feel about you if you don't call until Thursday?

When I don't have an answer or a resource for a potential client on the spot, I let them know when

I'll get back to them with an answer. Then, I make sure to keep that promise. Prospective clients are always impressed with my professionalism and trustworthiness because I remembered their need and followed up with it as promised.

Integrity also includes clearly communicating your boundaries and keeping them. As you are developing sales conversations, be sure that you are not over promising. I encourage my clients to set realistic expectations which will delight customers, and then, try to go one unexpected step further to amaze them. This is a great way to get referrals and maintain your reputation as a professional with high integrity.

You can accomplish this by careful attention to timelines. I recently had a new website designed. The web designer told me the project would require six weeks. Instead, it took twelve. Unfortunately, I was not amazed or delighted. When you promise anything to a client or prospect, ensure that you make promises you can keep.

Integrity has another facet. Always be certain that you are completely honest in everything. Today's consumers are extremely savvy. Many know how to do online research and may investigate you or the corporation you represent.

For example, I was considering hiring a new employee for one of my companies. One particular candidate had very impressive testimonials on his website. I sent an email to one of the people who provided an online testimonial to ask about the experience of working with this individual. I received a surprising reply. This man was astonished that he was publicized as a reference as he'd had a negative experience with the candidate and had not provided the glowing testimonial that was listed online with his name attached.

In our connected world, your reputation and integrity are even more important than in the past. It is very simple for prospects to contact your clients via email. So guard your reputation and cherish it for the treasure that it is.

#5 Stay Committed

There may come a day when you want to throw in the towel. Best-Selling Author and Speaker Jill Konrath tells of a time early in her sales career when she was selling photocopiers. She had an appointment to meet with the administrative assistant of a company president. However before the appointment, Jill read a sales training book which said a good salesperson would meet with decision makers, not assistants, so she then arranged a meeting with the company president instead.

When she arrived for the meeting with the president, the abandoned assistant was so angry that she launched into a tirade studded with four letter words. Jill fainted right there on the floor. When she awoke, she was helped to her feet and told to never return.

Some people may have quit the sales profession after such a dramatic event. Not Jill. She made the decision to learn from the experience and continue in sales, and as a result has had a brilliant sales and speaking career.

When you are in sales, you're going to have some tough days. Challenges will arise.

Top performers know that these challenges are part of selling. While you may not faint in front of a prospective client, you may make other glaring mistakes. It happens to the best of us. We are human after all.

When you feel like you've blown it, do your best to repair the damage with the prospect. When you can correct an error with honesty and great customer service, you may win a customer for life.

The most important things you can do are to move on and continue with your commitment to becoming a top performing salesperson.

#6 Find the Need

When you are in the midst of a sales conversation, it's your job to help the prospect determine if she wants what you have to offer. High performing salespeople do this by asking open-ended questions and listening carefully.

If you instead monopolize the conversation and blather on about the features and benefits of your service, you run the risk of overwhelming your prospect with too much information that isn't related to her needs and squelching any rising desire. I always like to begin a conversation with "I don't know if this is a fit but let's have a conversation and find out." It reminds me to keep the conversation a dialogue instead of a monologue. Plus, it takes the pressure off of both parties to sell or be sold.

People love to talk about themselves. The most successful sales conversations begin with your invitation to the prospect to tell her story.

It is important that you create a comfortable and safe environment for your prospect. You can do that by making the conversation all about them: their needs, challenges, vision, and hopes for the future.

When you ask an open-ended question like, "Tell me about what you've already tried to solve this problem," listen carefully for her needs.

By listening carefully and tailoring your responses specifically to the needs of that individual prospect, you can offer her exactly what she needs to move forward. This customization will create desire in your prospect, and desire is the first step towards yes!

#7 Know How to Handle a 'No'

My friend and fellow sales trainer, Julie Hansen, tells an amusing story about getting a big 'No' from a prospect. At the time, Julie sold advertising space in the National Enquirer. Julie worked hard to arrange a meeting with a brand director from Kraft Foods, the head of the Jell-O division.

Julie did an excellent sales presentation. However she got the sense that the brand manager was becoming increasingly uncomfortable. Finally Julie just asked if there was a reason why they were not moving forward.

The brand manager replied, "Well, don't you think Jell-O is a bit too up-scale for the Enquirer?"

Julie laughed and joked with the manager about being jilted by Jell-O. She then asked for and received a referral to another division of the company, which led to a successful contract.

High performing salespeople are not afraid to hear no. They know that a no may lead to another opportunity that is even better than the one at hand. Or, that the no may mean no for today but maybe for the future.

#8 Follow Up Fearlessly

When Sales Trainer Alice Kemper attended a trade show, she met a decision maker for a very large corporation, who seemed to be a perfect fit for the training she was selling. At his invitation, Alice flew to Chicago to present a proposal. The gentleman loved her proposal and added it to his division's corporate budget proposal.

Unfortunately, funding was not approved.

Alice did not give up. She faithfully called the decision maker every quarter for the next three years to follow up. He rarely returned her calls but seemed open to continue talking with Alice so she kept him on her follow up list.

Three years later he called her with full funding for her training program and Alice signed a very large contract.

Too many new salespeople stop following up too quickly, especially with qualified prospects, people who are the perfect fit for your product or service. Some sales take a very long time to develop, like Alice's large contract. Rainmakers know to continue following up with those prospects who are a perfect match for your offering.

The Power of Follow-Up

Done correctly, follow-up can maintain the relationship between you and your prospects. You are not following up to nag them into buying from you but to be their resource and to discuss ways you can solve their challenges and serve them.

Until you get a firm no, follow up creatively and help move the sales process forward.

If you neglect to follow up, someone else will and that person will get the business. I once attended a conference and sat next to a man who mentioned that he was in a coaching program led by a friend of mine. He was debating about continuing the coaching, as the investment seemed too high.

At the end of the conference, he excitedly told me that he'd committed to the conference presenter's year-long coaching program, which was five times more costly than the coaching he was doing with my colleague.

Why did this happen?

The conference presenter was at the top of this gentleman's mind when he was ready to make a decision. Something that the presenter said convinced the man to invest happily at a much higher price point. In sales, out of sight is often out of mind.

#9 Close the Sale

Many times you just need to ask for the business.

Prospects give subtle clues when they are ready to buy. High performing salespeople listen carefully for these signals and then ask for the business.

In the sales world, this is called the close. Sales training programs discuss different types of closes.

Once when I was selling books door to door for Southwestern, I had a lovely conversation with a young couple. I'd just had training on believing that people would want to buy my books so I said, "I'll be coming back to deliver your books at the end of the summer so let's write up the agreement now."

The couple asked me to wait while they left the room. I didn't know if I had offended them or what had happened.

When they returned to the room, they were smiling broadly. They told me they were both in sales and were so proud of me for using a technique called The Assumptive Close that they would be happy to buy books from me.

How did I have the courage to make this bold request?

I believed strongly in the merit of education and that the books I was selling would contribute positively to the educational level of each family. I liked this couple and wanted the best for their children. Most importantly, I listened carefully during our conversation and heard all the mini-yeses and clear buying signals they were giving me. I knew it was time to move the sale forward.

You can do the same!

#10 Be Yourself and Give Yourself Time

High performing salespeople embody their own uniqueness.

You don't have to be a cookie cutter or exact replica of me or any other high performing salesperson. Use your strengths and mix them with the skills and mindset you will learn in this book to develop your own style for sales success.

For example, you may be a meticulous record keeper, so you'll enjoy working with client relationship management programs and tracking forms to keep detailed metrics of your activities. Other salespeople may hate record keeping and depend on other ways to track their activities instead of a computerized program.

If you love to meet prospective clients at conferences or trade shows, make time in your schedule for as many conferences as you can. On the other hand, if you don't care for large crowds and feel more comfortable in a smaller setting, set up more individual meetings or make phone calls.

Determine what you do best and enjoy the most and use those strengths in your sales process. However if you are looking to increase your sales, I suggest looking for ways to get out of your comfort zone as well. If you don't stretch yourself and do the same things over and over with the same non-desired results, you don't grow.

Personally, I consider myself a bit of a maverick. I love coming up with new ways to sell. That's why the selling profession still interests me after all these years. There is an unlimited potential for personal innovation.

Can I Share Too Much of My Personal Life?

In certain selling situations, don't be afraid to get a little bit personal. If you have children or pets, feel free to share a few light-hearted stories about them, when you are talking with prospects. I've had many great conversations with prospective clients about hobbies, movies, books, and my children and pets. You don't need to share your entire life's story, but be willing to engage in friendly conversation as a way to establish a bond of trust.

When you "search" for similarities in opening up a conversation with your prospective client, you might be surprised how many you have in common and how effective it can be in the beginning of the selling process. For instance, "I have a Great Dane" or "I run marathons, too," may seem trivial. We often dismiss such things as "small talk." But that's a mistake. Similarity—the genuine, not manufactured variety is a key form of human connection. When common ground is shared, prospects are more likely to move toward you.

However, it is important to be aware of your potential client's buying personality. Many are on a tight time schedule and will want you to get right to the point and disregard small talk. When I sold medical equipment to physicians this was often the case. I became adept at walking and talking. Often times I had only a few minutes between patients to find out the physician's need. I was well prepared with questions and moved the sales process forward by qualifying and looking for a fit in the initial conversation.

Use your keen listening skills and you'll be able to sense if your prospect will enjoy hearing your personal stories or not.

Give Yourself Time

Rainmaker sales professions are not born, they develop over time. In fact, the more time you spend in selling conversations, the more skill you will develop. In Malcolm Gladwell's book *Outliers*, he suggests that if you engage in an activity for 10,000 hours, you will become an expert. That may sound like an impossible goal but you can reach it quickly by immersing yourself in sales conversations.

Don't expect to be perfect from the start of your sales career. Whether you are just beginning to sell or have been at it for a while, your skills and expertise will grow over time.

Chapter 3
Building Your Rainmaker Mindset

"Success seems to be connected with action. Successful people keep moving. They make mistakes but don't quit."

~ Conrad Hilton

Sales are the lifeblood of every business. Whether you are selling for a large corporation or for your own business, you are creating the future of that business by selling. Without a steady stream of sales, a company will wither, just like a plant without enough water.

In 2004, during my years as a national top performer in medical sales, my sales manager, Monica Llano, gave me a book called *How to be a Rainmaker* by Jeffrey J. Fox, and wrote on the inside cover, "Carolyn, You are a Rainmaker!" This book sits prominently on my desk and reminds me of what I had worked for so diligently for many years.

A Rainmaker is passionate and bold about selling, using a set of highly developed skills in communication, listening and problem solving.

You become a rainmaker over time as you learn new skills in the sales process along with the personal characteristics, which support you in giving your best to your prospects. Rainmakers are:

- Resilient
- Persistent
- Creative
- Optimistic
- Passionate
- Bold communicators
- Honest and full of personal integrity
- Open to try new things
- Action oriented and energetic
- Eager to reach goals
- Confident leaders
- Happy to meet new people and find ways to serve them
- Resourceful
- Great storytellers

To become a rainmaker, a high performing sales professional, you really need just two things:

- Outstanding relationship building skills
- A mindset focused on reaching and exceeding your goals

When you have these two ingredients in place, you will naturally succeed at selling.

When I first started selling books door to door, I was not very skilled. I made almost no sales during that difficult first week. I could have easily given up and gone back home in defeat. However, I was committed to succeeding and willing to learn.

I got better and better at making sales and by the end of the first summer, I was invited to become a sales manager and mentor to new student teams. Over time, with support, training and practice, I'd mastered the ability to reach and exceed my sales goals.

If you are not selling as successfully as you wish today, you can learn the skills you need as long as you are willing to stretch out of your comfort zone and have fun trying new things until you find the techniques that work well for you.

Since your first sale is always to yourself, let's focus on strengthening your rainmaker mindset first before we dive into some of the specific rainmaker sales skills.

You are Not an Interruption

One of the biggest challenges I observe when working with new salespeople is the feeling that they are an interruption or bothering their prospect. This happens in face-to-face selling when the salesperson apologizes for stopping by with information. During phone sales, this feeling of interruption can cause you to speak too quickly and rush the prospect with an assumption of getting a no. If you've ever said, "I know you are busy so let me just tell you about this quickly," you've lost sight of the value you bring to the lives of your customers.

What you have to offer is important. People want to know about your products or services. You are not interrupting or bothering a prospect, you are discovering if there is an opportunity to help. I position myself as a valued resource and this puts me on a level playing field with my prospects.

Recently I accompanied my client Brandon on his daily sales calls to medical offices. Brandon was frustrated with his sales numbers and wanted to discover what he was doing to block sales.

After a few calls, it was easy to see why he was getting nowhere fast. Each time he went in to see a prospect, he was stopped by a receptionist. His posture, tone of voice, and mannerisms communicated the message that he just knew the office was busy that day and that he was sorry for being a nuisance. Brandon made it easy for the receptionist to turn him down.

I took him to coffee and we did a role play where I demonstrated how I would approach the receptionist with confidence, certain that my prospect would be so delighted to see me she would thank her receptionist for introducing us.

When Brandon observed this difference, he immediately shifted his mindset and his approach. He had a stellar afternoon, setting up appointments, holding an impromptu meeting and generating a feeling of positive momentum. I asked him what he learned from this experience. He said,

1. Make the gatekeeper an ally, not an enemy. (NOTE- in sales we often call receptionists or assistants gatekeepers)

2. Engage, don't evade. Engage the gatekeeper so that they have a positive and friendly attitude towards you.

3. If you are nervous, stressed or tense, you will transfer those feelings to your voice, your behavior and choice of words. Smile and confidently greet everyone with energy and ease.

4. Ask and you shall receive.

Rainmakers Never Pre-Judge

I once worked with a woman who sold cars. One day a man walked into the dealership with tattered clothes and blood dripping down his forehead. No one wanted to talk with him so she got him a bandage, gave him something to drink, and ended up selling him a top-of- the-line truck.

You can never judge a prospect by appearance or assume they can't afford what you are offering. Rainmakers know that people find money for what they really value and that appearances are often deceiving.

Aim to serve each person you encounter and give him the opportunity to decide on your offer.

Make Prospects the Star

Rainmakers know that selling is not about them, it is about the person in front of them. Find ways to make your prospect shine in each conversation. One of the best ways to do this is to ask open-ended questions such as:

- What do you think about _____?
- What's your biggest vision for this?
- Can you share a few successes you've already created?

In our busy world, people are rarely asked these kinds of questions. When you follow a question like this with deep listening and your full attention, your prospect will be honored and enjoy the conversation greatly.

Your goal is not to make a one-time sale, but to become a trusted advisor to your prospect. Take the time to build a long-term relationship with your prospects and customers by genuinely getting to know each of them. When you have your prospect's best interests at heart and make them feel safe with you, your prospects will appreciate you and your expertise deeply, and feel good about buying from you.

Adapt to Your Prospect's Pace

It is important to remember that your prospects are intelligent, capable people who can draw their own conclusions about your offer. Rather than rushing someone with a high pressure stock selling script, adapt your tone, pace, and presentation to the style of your prospect.

People buy at different speeds. For example, I tend to make quick decisions when purchasing. My husband makes decisions slowly and carefully after he learns all the facts. If a salesperson approached us both in the same fashion without taking the time to adapt to our varying buying speeds, one of us would not be well served and would probably say no to what is offered.

Rainmakers are Pleasantly Persistent

I was working with a challenging prospective client recently. We had several conversations and emails which were moving in the direction of a sale and then suddenly he stopped returning my calls and replying to my emails.

I remained pleasantly persistent, kept him on my follow up list, and stayed on his radar. I gave him some space but continued to follow up whenever I had something I thought he would be interested in.

When I sent him an article regarding time management for his sales managers, a problem we'd discussed earlier, I finally got a response. He sent me an email apologizing for not returning my calls or answering my emails. He said, "I'm probably your worst nightmare. Being busy is no excuse and I sincerely apologize."

Rather than becoming frustrated with his pace or giving up on him, I assured him that I appreciated the time we had in that moment. Then I suggested that to save time, we schedule a follow up call now rather than trying to fit it in later. In the next call we moved forward with a coaching contract.

Because I adjusted my schedule to mesh with his, this prospect became a very happy client. There was no need to beg and plead for his time or 'just check in with him.'

Rainmakers have the ability to patiently wait for a yes and persevere to get one whenever possible.

Inspiration Leads to Yes

Your prospects want to be inspired. They are searching for solutions and answers.

When you can lead prospects in a discussion about their goals and aspirations, and then provide resources to help them achieve those goals, you paint a picture of what could be possible for them. In our world of stress, frustrations, and negativity, just imagine how refreshing a conversation about a positive future will feel to your prospects.

Some sales training programs encourage dwelling on prospects' pain points. In my experience, it is more effective to inspire someone with a focus on positive goals than to spend the bulk of a sales conversation on what's not working. If the conversation is steered toward the problems then it's important to ask questions about creating solutions, which will fix the perceived problems.

Here are some questions you may ask to steer the conversation towards the future as well as give the prospect the opportunity to share some of her challenges:

1. What would life be like if you did not have this challenge?

2. What have you already tried?

3. What resources do you have to address this challenge?

When you have a positive, optimistic mindset for yourself and for your clients, you empower them during your conversations and increase their belief in their capacities. They will sense your positive regard for them and your heartfelt respect.

We all know that people buy from those they know, like and trust. I've discovered that people want to enjoy the process of making a purchase as well as the relationship with the person making the sale. In a recent survey conducted by The Corporate Executive Board, respondents listed these reasons why they buy from and stay loyal to a company:

19% – Company/brand impact
19% – Product and service delivery
9% – Value-to-price ratio
53% – The sales experience

Rainmakers realize that creating a positive, empowering, and inspiring relationship with a prospect makes the sales experience enjoyable for everyone. It really is all about your level of caring and positive regard for the person in front of you, whether that is a CEO, a work-at-home mom, or a receptionist. When you inspire, you serve. That service is at the heart of selling success.

Rainmakers Realize that Failure is Just Part of the Sales Landscape

Zig Ziglar said it best, "Remember that failure is an event, not a person." In my thirty years of selling, I've noticed that people who succeed are those who are willing to experiment and learn from every experience, win or lose.

There will be days when you strike out, deals that will fall apart at the final moments, and prospects, who buy from competitors instead of from you. That's okay.

In my first sales job, I remember some days where I totally struck out. Just imagine thirteen straight hours of knocking on doors with twenty-five to thirty sales conversations and not one sale. Ouch!

However, there were also days, after I learned my craft, when 100% of my sales conversations led to a sale. On those days I felt magical. On one beautiful, golden day I had 17 consecutive sales calls and all 17 prospects bought. I'll never forget the rush of pride and excitement I felt on that day. Each conversation and sale built momentum for the next, and it became a game to see how long I could keep it going.

I learned many important skills from both the goose-egg days and the golden days. You will find this is true in your sales career too. Each sales experience adds to your skill and knowledge. You always have the opportunity to refine your approach and evolve your selling skills.

Rainmakers are not born....they grow. You'll grow too.

Let's Take A Look

Ready to access your rainmaker sales skills? I'd like you to complete a brief assessment now so you can identify your current strengths and areas where you can grow.

Please go to **http://rainmakermindset.com/ readerbonus/** readerbonus and download a copy of my Rainmaker Sales Assessment. Complete it as honestly as you can. Do this assessment before you read any further in the book.

Assessment:

I have written goals for myself.

Less True   More True
  1   2   3   4   5

I have a positive outlook and attitude.

Less True   More True
  1   2   3   4   5

I have created and implemented an effective sales process.

Less True   More True
1   2   3   4   5

I know the winning formula for my sales success.

Less True   More True
1   2   3   4   5

I am a problem solver and create my own solutions.

Less True   More True
1   2   3   4   5

I can clearly identify my rainmaker qualities.

Less True   More True
1   2   3   4   5

I hold myself accountable for my results and my life.

Less True   More True
1   2   3   4   5

I strategize and plan my goals for each week.

Less True   More True
1   2   3   4   5

I am able to identify the weak spots in my selling process.

Less True   More True
1   2   3   4   5

I am effective at executing what I learn from sales training, meetings and coaching.

Less True   More True
 1   2   3   4   5

I utilize a sales automated system (CRM) effectively.

Less True   More True
 1   2   3   4   5

I am consistently building my pipeline as well as effectively managing my current accounts.

Less True   More True
 1   2   3   4   5

I utilize role-play to improve my sales conversations and presentations.

Less True   More True
 1   2   3   4   5

I know my closing ratios.

Less True   More True
 1   2   3   4   5

I am effective at getting commitments from my prospects to move the sales process forward.

Less True   More True
 1   2   3   4   5

I know exactly what I need to do to achieve my long- and short-term goals for growth.

Less True   More True
 1   2   3   4   5

I know exactly what training, development and coaching it will take to achieve my sales goals and grow my skills.

Less True   More True
  1   2   3   4   5

Bonus tip: Use this assessment to monitor your progress. Tuck your completed assessment with today's date into the back of this book. Then, place a note on your calendar to re-take the assessment in 30 days, after you have completed the assessment and started to implement the specific skills you've discovered in this book.

I'd love to hear how your scores have increased!

Email me at Carolyn@RainMakerMindset.com

SECTION 2
The Sales Process

I'll always be grateful to the Southwestern Company for teaching me how to sell. When I was a scared college kid, they taught me a basic sales process, which enabled me to make sales consistently and confidently. The process was so successful that I was able to pay for my college expenses, travel around the world and create a career as a professional salesperson, selling everything from high-end capital medical equipment, to training programs, to my personal sales coaching services.

I learned that it does not matter what you are selling; without a clear sales process, you will struggle to sell something as inexpensive as a children's book or as costly as a multi-million dollar piece of equipment.

Whether you are brand new to sales, or you've been selling for a long time and want to improve your success rate, you will benefit from having a clear sales process to guide all your conversations.

What I See in the Trenches

I often accompany new salespeople out in the field on sales calls or observe them making telephone sales calls. The most common errors I observe come from stress. The new coach will blather on and on about the features of her coaching program without letting the prospective client put a word in edgewise. The new sales rep will timidly approach a gatekeeper and apologetically ask to leave a brochure for the physician. The new telephone sales associate will rush to close a sale in the first two minutes of a call because he feels pressure to meet a quota.

A Process Gives You Confidence

Let me share my rainmaker sales process, which I developed over my thirty years of selling and training. This five-step process honors the prospect as well as the person who is selling. It is natural, conversational and effective whether you are selling a physical product or an intangible service such as coaching or consulting. It does not rely on a stale, canned script or high pressured tactics which make everyone feel uncomfortable and stressed out.

The goal of the rainmaker selling process is to connect deeply and respectfully with your prospect, and then collaborate on a solution that meets his needs. Deeply rooted in the rainmaker mindset, this process depends on the integrity and honesty of the sales professional and makes the process of selling enjoyable for both parties.

The Rainmaker Sales Process

- **Step 1 -** Keep a full pipeline of prospects so that you have a feeling of abundance and are not feeling the pressure to "sell" everyone you meet.
- **Step 2 -** Establish rapport so that you have a level of trust with your prospect. Share stories, be vulnerable, and listen deeply. Ask for a commitment (close) for the next step.

- **Step 3** - Ask powerful questions, listen for needs and qualify your prospect so you don't waste anyone's time. Qualify and ask for a commitment (close) for the next step.
- **Step 4** - Present your product/service. Keep this a dialogue instead of a monologue. Meet the needs of your prospect by co-creating an individualized solution, then asking for a commitment to move the sales process forward. Be a valuable resource.
- **Step 5** - Close and solidify the sale and ask for referrals.

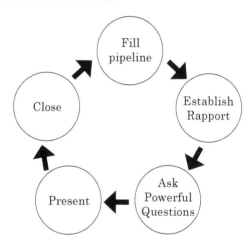

When you combine my rainmaker sales process with your own personality and communication style, you'll enjoy hearing yes more often, great relationships with your customers, and a stellar reputation in your marketplace.

Let's look at each step in depth so you can learn to implement each of them naturally.

Chapter 4
Filling the Pipeline

"All successful people, men and women, are big dreamers. They imagine what their future could be, ideal in every respect, and then they work every day toward their distant vision, that goal or purpose."

~ Brian Tracy

In order to have a feeling of abundance instead of fear and lack, it's important to keep a steady stream of potential clients in your pipeline. The more people you encounter, the more prospects flow into your pipeline.

You can build your pipeline in many ways. You may schedule a meeting at corporations, meet prospects for coffee, attend trade shows or conferences; use social media, join a networking group, do presentations or teleclasses, volunteer in your community or attend charity events.

You never know when you will meet someone who needs your services. If you are curious, friendly, and a skillful listener, you can find new people to add to your pipeline everywhere you go.

One of my clients, Ann, is a new coach who has attracted 35 new clients in a few short months. She has the gift of being able to see opportunities in everyday conversations. Ann has a way of asking whomever she's in front of about their passion, which is so engaging that they can't help but ask her about what she does as well, opening the door for her to share about her work.

Ann had some medical issues recently, which required home health nursing. When the nurse arrived, she asked about her work. Ann said "I'd love to tell all about it but first, tell me about you."

The nurse shared her dream of moving to Germany and working as a nurse. Ann asked more questions and the nurse shared her challenges in achieving her dream. They brainstormed some ways to reach her goals and by the end of the discussion, her nurse was excited about her future. She asked Ann more about her life coaching work and by the end of their appointment, she had hired Ann as her coach.

Prospecting in Your Neighborhood

I have a big dog, a Great Dane named Lilly Kate. When I walk Lilly Kate, most people cross to the other side of the street. However, one guy in my neighborhood has another large dog, a bull mastiff. One morning I was out with Lilly Kate and this fellow started talking with me about the joys of owning big dogs. We decided to walk together for a bit and let our dogs enjoy each other.

We walked and talked. I asked him what he did and he started to tell me all about his rapidly expanding apparel company. He'd hired his first salesperson and was wondering how to best delegate some of the things on his plate to this new employee.

When he asked me what I did, I briefly mentioned that I work with the best clients in the world as a sales coach and mentioned I was working on my delegating skills too. Then I turned the conversation back to him. At the end of our walk, we exchanged cards and talked about meeting again at the dog park.

You may be wondering why I did not try to sell him sales coaching for his new staff member. Did I miss an opportunity?

Not at all. This man lives right down the street from me. I'll see him again. Since we'd just met, there was no need to try to sell him something. We hadn't discussed what his needs were yet. Instead, now that I know him and that he has a new salesperson; he becomes part of my pipeline of potential clients.

The point of these two stories is that you never know when you will encounter a prospective client. When you are curious, friendly, and alert to the possibilities that come your way, you will continually add people to your pipeline.

However, don't leave your pipeline to chance. Proactively create opportunities to encounter potential prospects at industry events, networking meetings, community events, and online in forums or social media networks. Determine where your potential prospects gather, in person or virtually, and spend time in those places as often as possible.

Be bold and open conversations with people.

"Fortune favors the bold." -Virgil

When I was in college, after I had spent a summer doing door-to-door sales, Lauren Bacall came to our campus to participate in a large event. I was enamored with her; she was my favorite actress back then. I loved her sense of style and confidence. I was thrilled to see her in person and thought it would be great to get her autograph.

The event on campus was held outdoors in a large grassy area. Thousands of people were there listening to the presentations.

After her presentation, I noticed Ms. Bacall going into the student center while another speaker started his speech. I decided to follow her and ended up tailing her right into the restroom.

There I was, standing outside her stall. I said, "Ms. Bacall, I'm such a huge fan of yours. Would you mind giving me an autograph?"

I'll never forget her reply. She chuckled and replied in her distinctive deep voice, "Would you mind? I'll be happy to sign your autograph but I'd first like to finish in here and wash my hands."

In a few minutes we had a short conversation; she gave me an autograph, and then went on her way. That day I approached someone who had the power to intimidate me. It was a little scary but I realized I'd never get another opportunity like this so I had to be bold and just ask.

That experience taught me that it was okay to open up conversations with people. This skill is a tremendous asset in sales. When you can easily start a conversation with a prospective client, you are on the road to a successful sale.

One of the best ways to do this is to ask questions. People love to talk about themselves. Often, you only need to start the conversation rolling with an engaging, open-ended question.

Some of my favorite conversation starters for individual meetings:

- I'd love to hear your story.
- What do you think about _____?
- How did you begin _____?
- What's your vision for your business?

However, I've learned that there is a difference between starting a conversation with an individual prospect and getting a good conversation going in a multi-person meeting. When you are opening a conversation in a group, it is important to encourage everyone to participate in the conversation. You may have to steer the conversation just a bit to ensure that no one is just sitting quietly for too long.

Use these ideas for opening conversations in multi-person corporate meetings, tailoring your questions based on your preparatory research.

- Ask open-ended questions (who, what, where, when, why, how, how much, tell me about it, describe for me)
- What is the corporate structure?
- Determine each participant's role at the company. (This is an excellent question to address to each participant and draw out those people who have not yet spoken.)
- Ask what's important and interesting to each of them.
- Learn about their short and long term goals.
- Discuss any risks they see in their future.
- Ask how industry trends are impacting their company.

For each of these potential discussion areas, be sure to echo back what you've heard and encourage speakers to expand, elaborate, and go into further detail about each answer. Remember, these conversations will help you learn how to create a solution for each client that fits his needs perfectly!

Monitor Reactions

It is very important to pay close attention to the verbal and nonverbal cues people send. For example, when I am at a networking meeting, I try to encourage my conversational partner to speak first by asking a question. Then, I listen carefully and watch his body language to gauge how open he is to talking with me. If he gives a very clipped answer, glances away or crosses his arms, I know he is not ready for a long conversation.

Recently, I was doing a presentation at a large conference. My co-presenter and I were standing outside the door of our presentation room with all our materials in our arms, waiting to go in and prepare the room.

A man came up to us and tried to open a conversation with us. He started telling us about his product and why we should buy it. When we mentioned that we were speaking in a few minutes and needed time to prepare, he spoke louder and faster about why we should say yes to his product.

He was not a rainmaker sales professional!

When you meet people for the first time, your only goal is to connect with them. You may discover a potential client lead or a new friend but will not make any progress if your focus is on selling.

Special Techniques for Networking Events

Have you ever attended a networking event and felt overwhelmed or like you were surrounded by a flock of hungry vultures?

I often observe others shoving their business cards in peoples' faces, not even asking if they'd like one. It's as if they are in a contest to see how many people they can meet and how many of their cards they can get rid of. This is not being a rainmaker sales professional but being a pest!

When I attend networking events, my goal is to have great conversations with a few people and, if there seems to be a fit between us, request their business card so that I can follow up with them.

Instead of stressing out trying to meet everyone present, if you use my method of connecting deeply with just a few people who seem to be a fit, you will create a pipeline of new and quality prospects while you enjoy the process. Quality is much better than quantity when it comes to prospects.

Your Current Customers Can Add to Your Pipeline

Your existing customers can be your best source of prospects for your pipeline. Ask regularly for suggestions of the names of people they know who could benefit from the same type of work that you are doing together.

When I was in medical sales, I would always ask my clients for referrals to other physicians who could benefit from the learning about the medical equipment services I offered. These referrals opened many doors for me.

I recently attended a networking meeting in Los Angeles with a clear goal in mind. I wanted to meet with the host to open the door to a future speaking engagement for that group. Everything fell into place beautifully. One of my former clients was at the meeting and gave me an unsolicited glowing recommendation in the introduction section of the meeting. When I connected with the host at the end of the meeting, she was very enthusiastic about scheduling a speaking event.

There is only one caveat: You must promise to always follow up in a timely manner on any leads or referrals from current clients, even if you are tired or busy.

Don't forget to thank your referral sources. I like sending handwritten thank you cards. In our world of email and text messages, an old-fashioned handwritten note is memorable and appreciated.

Recently I was meeting with a CEO of a large corporation. In the course of our conversation, he mentioned he was turning 50 the following week. After our meeting I got a birthday card specifically for 50th birthdays and sent it to him as a thank you for our meeting. He was so surprised he called to thank me and to set up another meeting to discuss working together.

Handwritten cards and notes work precisely because few people take time to write them any longer. Rainmakers do!

Don't Give Up Too Soon

When I was starting in medical sales, I was having a tough time in a new territory. I had a rough day with no success at all, not even to schedule an appointment. I was feeling pretty crummy and decided I'd go to the movies after I finished the last call so that I could forget about that miserable day.

My final call was with a pain management physician. We discussed my company's medical devices and he decided he couldn't use any of the devices I had to offer. Another no!

At the very end of our conversation, he mentioned the name of an orthopedic surgeon who might be interested in the equipment. I had a choice to make. Should I give up and go to the movies or find a pay phone (yes, this was before cell phones were commonplace) and make one more call?

I decided to save the movie for later and to make that call. The surgeon I contacted was so interested that he asked me to come right over to his office for a meeting that afternoon. He was delighted to see the devices and became a client on the spot.

That surgeon became my top referring physician for the next ten years and led me to several additional large contracts. You never know where the power of one referral will take you, especially if you refuse to give up and quit too early.

"Word of Mouth" Referrals are Powerful

The first summer I sold books door-to-door, I started a notebook I labeled "Families for Education." Whenever I sold books to a family,

I'd ask them to write a short statement in my book about why they felt education was so important.

This book became a wonderful sales tool. When I called on a new family, I showed them my book with testimonials from people in their community who had happily invested in books for their children and grandchildren's education.

You can easily replicate this idea. Ask for testimonials from satisfied customers and use them to demonstrate the value of your work without having to brag. You can use these testimonials in your marketing materials, on your website, and in follow-up emails. An endorsement is a powerful tool for opening doors.

Prioritize Your Prospects

Once you have some potential customers in your pipeline, you'll find it helpful to keep a record of them in a database, on a spreadsheet, or use a Customer Relationship Management (CRM) system. This will enable you to rank each person in your pipeline. Use a simple A, B, C system, rating each person's potential as a future client.

Then, give your A prospects your greatest level of attention. When you concentrate your attention on your warmest leads, you will maximize your time and your profits. Be sure to spend some time on your B and C prospects as well.

Create a system where you review your prospect list on a weekly basis and update your rankings. I like to do this at the end of every week, updating my CRM program with any notes or new information I gathered during the week as well as the outcome of any follow up activity.

Cold Calling

In the sales training world, a distinction is made between warm calls and cold calls. A warm call is to someone you may have already met, perhaps at a networking event or in person, or someone to whom you've been introduced. A cold call is to someone who is a stranger to you at the moment. You may have the opportunity to make a cold call if you work in corporate sales or if you are following up on a lead from someone you know.

When I sold medical devices to physicians, I would make cold calls to offices that had no idea my company existed until I arrived. My work selling books door-to-door was exclusively with cold calls.

Cold calls require a different approach than warm calls. Your first task with a cold call is often to get past a gatekeeper to speak with someone who can make buying decisions. In the corporate setting, gatekeepers are generally executive assistants or receptionists. In a doctors' office it may be the doctor's wife or mother. Often, they are instructed to keep all salespeople away from the decision makers, so it can be a challenge to work with them. But they can become your most trusted ally and best friend. Gatekeepers are there to keep out the time wasters and the bad guys. You are not either of these people.

My colleague and fellow sales trainer Lori Richardson recalls a time when she was trying to meet with the Chief Financial Officer of a corporation. She placed several calls to his assistant who was not at all friendly. In fact, the assistant rudely told Lori to never contact the company again. Some months later, the CFO called Lori's firm and asked for a meeting.

Rainmakers realize that the gatekeeper is not the person who should make decisions for an entire corporation. It may require some creativity to get past the gatekeeper and get an appointment with someone who can make those decisions, but it is a worthwhile pursuit.

Keith Rosen, a pioneer of management coach training, suggests that you think of the gatekeeper as a concierge. Instead of focusing on getting through the gatekeeper, shift your mindset to making friends with the concierge. Consider this for a moment. A concierge wants to help you. The only caveat is you have to give them a reason to do so.

However, don't automatically judge all gatekeepers as your enemy. Babette Ten Haken, of SalesAerobics.com once had a meeting scheduled with a CEO from a manufacturing firm. When she arrived, the front desk receptionist told her he was not in. However, Babette knew he was in his office, she could see him in his glassed-in office.

Babette rescheduled the meeting. When she arrived the second time, the same thing happened. While she knew the CEO was in his office, the receptionist looked her right in the eye and said he was not there.

Babette took the young woman aside and asked her if she liked what she was doing and if she felt good about working for a boss who forced her to lie and behave unethically. Babette could see the CEO listening to her conversation with the receptionist and boldly spoke about her personal ethics and the importance of staying true to your core values. Two weeks later the young woman called Babette and thanked her for helping her see she needed to move on to a more ethical work situation.

That story illustrates the fact that gatekeepers are human. You never know if they are blocking your access to a decision maker because they have been instructed to do so or if they are trying to protect their supervisor from an interruption.

When you approach a gatekeeper, be prepared to be friendly, positive, and clearly state the benefit of your information to the company and to the individual you are trying to see. Use your relationship building skills to create rapport with the gatekeeper and graciously thank her for her time and assistance.

Sometimes you need to be boldly creative and work around a gatekeeper who is blocking you. When I was doing a field sales ride-along with one of my coaching clients, Bill, he was getting nowhere with a particular caseworker at a large hospital. This caseworker did not want any of his information and was not willing to connect him to anyone else.

Bill knew that he had valuable information for the hospital staff and physicians who treated elderly patients. Bill and I brainstormed and realized that most of the people who would need his information worked in a different department from the caseworker who was causing the challenge.

So, we tried another avenue. We went to the emergency room front desk and asked to see one of the caseworkers who worked with seniors needing emergency care. The caseworker in the ER was delighted to meet us and grateful for the information. He enthusiastically agreed to Bill's offer for a staff training session. This meeting led to several other training referrals and introductions within the same hospital. Because Bill did not let the first gatekeeper stop him, he was able to create a very strong connection to this hospital and many referrals for his company.

When There is No Gatekeeper

What if you are cold calling on people who don't have a gatekeeper? If you sell professional coaching, healing services, consulting, or products to solopreneurs, there won't be a gatekeeper who gets in your way. Your challenge there will be the pull of the status quo and your prospect's internal resistance to change. In these situations, your skills in building relationships will be crucial to your selling success.

Let's dive into the rainmaker approach for establishing authentic, real rapport right away.

Chapter 5
Establish and Maintain Rapport

"If you once forfeit the confidence of your fellow citizens, you can never regain their respect and esteem. It is true that you may fool all of the people some of the time; you can even fool some of the people all of the time; but you can't fool all of the people all of the time."
~ Abraham Lincoln, *Speech at Clinton, Illinois, September 8, 1854*

Gail, a brand new career coach, called me in a panic. She attended a local chamber of commerce meeting and gave her elevator speech about helping employees manage career transition. A gentleman at her lunch table loved what she had to say and booked an appointment with her to meet for coffee and discuss her work. He mentioned he was in a new position and feeling like he needed help bonding with his new employees.

Gail was thrilled and terrified. She called to ask me how to conduct herself in that first meeting so that she could sell coaching services to the gentleman.

The first interaction with a prospective client sets the tone for the entire relationship. Done right, you can establish a trusting and enjoyable working relationship. Done wrong, you risk alienating a prospect and losing a sale.

Like always, I suggest you take a rainmaker approach to this initial meeting, combing your confidence and very best people skills. Your goal is to build a lasting, positive relationship with your prospect, so establishing a strong initial rapport is a key strategy.

Before the Meeting: Evaluate Your Opportunity and Determine Your Timeline

When I sold books door-to-door, I usually had only one chance to make a sale so I had to learn to quickly establish rapport. I had about twenty to thirty minutes to spend with each family: to find a need, fulfill it and close.

Later in my sales career, I sold high-ticket items and services and had several meetings before any sales occurred. Today, when I sell coaching services, there are times when I close a sale in one phone call, and other times where a series of calls or face-to-face meetings are completed before the sale.

The first step for you is to decide how likely it will be to create a sale from this first meeting. Ask yourself:

- Is this your only opportunity to speak with the prospect or is it an initial meeting that will be followed with additional interactions?
- Who are all of the decision makers? Are they in the room and if not, how will this information be relayed to them?

This information will determine your pace and agenda for your initial meeting. If you feel that this could be a single situation sale, you will set a pace to move through your sales process in that meeting. If this is just an initial meeting, slow down and continue to build rapport.

Either way, your primary goal in an initial meeting is to build rapport, (and) begin a lasting, positive relationship with your prospect and find out if there's a fit.

Multiple Decision Makers

Working with multiple decision makers can pose some special challenges. One of my clients recently asked for my help in shortening his sales cycle. It was taking six to nine months for him to close a sale because there were so many decision makers involved in the process. After some brainstorming, we created a step-by-step process to build rapport with all the decision makers and a process to provide continuous follow up for each of them. This effort was very successful in shortening the sales cycles. The key to his new success was getting everyone on board in the rapport stage.

I've created a checklist which will help you prepare for effective meetings. Download your copy at **http://rainmakermindset.com/readerbonus/**

The Rainmaker Rapport Building Process

Step 1- Open the Conversation

If appropriate, begin your conversation with some small talk. I like to ask about hobbies, books, community events or a new movie. Keep the conversation light and fun. It is important for you to be fully present and listen to the conversation, not just wait to pounce on the prospect and tell them all about your product or service.

I recently had an initial lunch meeting with a corporate director. We started chatting and he mentioned that he was training for a triathlon. He was so excited that his entire face lit up when he talked about it. He said something very important, that the training for a triathlon began the moment you signed up for a race.

This told me some very important things about him. I realized he understood the importance of training and of making a commitment to achieving a goal. These concepts helped me understand some of his values and how to speak his language when I told him about my corporate training and coaching programs.

Continue the general conversation until you've learned a bit about the person and you've been able to share something about yourself as well. In time, you'll be able to sense when you started a connection and the time is right to move the conversation forward.

Aim to make your prospect smile. Watch for lively eye contact, leaning in, and a relaxed posture. Those signals tell you that she is relaxed and enjoying the conversation. Also be aware of your body language – smile, stand tall and when sitting, sit back to remind yourself to be in listening mode not selling mode.

When Your Prospect Does Not Want to Chat

Sometimes your prospect will not respond well to these rapport building questions. This can be very intimidating, especially if you begin to worry that he does not like you or regrets agreeing to this meeting with you.

Before you give up, just remember that some people are very focused and do not enjoy general conversation. Or he may be extremely busy, stressed, or have a pressing problem on his mind.

If you find that your prospect is reluctant to share much information, try sharing a story of your own and demonstrate some vulnerability. You could also use a story about one of your clients. These stories will often open the floodgates and your prospect will feel comfortable sharing challenges and desires.

Find a story that highlights the value of your offer. I had a woman contact me recently regarding sales coaching. In our initial conversation I asked her to share her vision, goals and dreams. I put the spotlight on her and allowed her to shine. She was considering a transition from account support to sales, and she had a lot of doubts.

When the space opened up, I asked if I could share my transition story. She was all ears. I told her about the time I was considering leaving a high paying medical sales job to branch out on my own and start my own coaching business. I shared that I had some huge doubts and fears about pulling it off. My story resonated with the woman and allowed her to share her current frustrations with her job and fears about her career transition. We had a great connection, so I invited her to a follow up session. In that conversation, I had her visualize where she would be if she stayed in status quo and where she would be if she got out of her comfort zone. By the end of that second call, she was asking me which coaching package she should begin with. She sold herself on why she wanted to move forward.

Think back over your career and personal life for some stories that you could share to build rapport. Write them out and practice telling them so that you can tell them in a concise and engaging manner. Be sure you have a clear point in each story that you can tie into your offer.

When you take time to prepare a few stories ahead of time, you'll be able to confidently tell them whenever you need a way to get a prospect to open up to you.

Step 2- Hear the Story

After you have built some initial personal rapport with your prospect, ask your prospect an open-ended question related to his business or profession.

Questions help you establish rapport, build quality relationships, differentiate you to your prospects, and show that you take a genuine interest in them.

Some of my favorites are:

- Tell me about your work/business/company.
- What do you think about _____?
- I'd love to hear the story of how you got where you are today.
- How do you feel about the service you are getting from your current provider?
- What is your status in terms of looking to make a change?
- What are some challenges that you are experiencing?

For more information on creating powerful questions, I highly recommend *Power Questions by* Andrew Sobol. I believe this book should be recommended reading for all sales professionals. Sales success depends on the ability to ask powerful and open-ended questions.

However, powerful questions are only effective if they are combined with authentic listening. At this stage in the process, it is important for you to listen deeply and let your prospect speak.

People love to talk about themselves. Good listeners are rare. When your prospect sees that you are genuinely interested and listening deeply, rapport will be created.

It seems simple, but listening is an overlooked but vital ingredient in successful selling. The more you listen and the less you speak in this stage, the more sales you will close.

Step 3- Hear and Remark on Star Qualities

As you listen to the story of your prospect, listen for things like courage, creativity, leadership, strength, or honor. Remark on those positive qualities or virtues. Often, people don't realize that they possess admirable qualities. When you can highlight those qualities, you empower your prospect. Do this sincerely, from your heart, and you will be trusted and liked.

Choice point:
Continue or set the next meeting
Now that you have established rapport, you will need to decide if you will make an offer in

this conversation or move forward by setting up another meeting. Remember how I encouraged you to plan your agenda before the meeting? At this point in the conversation, you'll proceed in one of two directions based on your pre-meeting plan and the results of your rapport building conversation.

Path 1: Move Forward to the Sale

If you are in a single meeting sales process, begin asking additional questions about what your prospect needs. Discover what he has already tried, what is working well, and where he needs support.

Again, you will listen more than you speak here. Your goal is to identify needs and understand the nuances of your prospect's situation. Then you'll continue the steps in your sales process.

Path 2: The Multi-Step Meeting Process

If you are in multi-step meeting process, the goal of this initial session was to establish rapport. At this point in the meeting, explore logical next steps with your prospect, which may include:

- Discussing if any other participants should be included in this discussion
- When to meet again to continue the discussion

Rapport Requires Follow Up

Rapport was established in your meeting and it requires nurturing to grow and deepen. After your first meeting, be sure to send a personalized follow-up within twenty-four hours. I like to challenge myself to do it immediately after the meeting.

This is fun!

Follow-up can be as simple as a handwritten thank you note, an email with a resource or even a recommendation for a great movie.

Creating the perfect follow-up process is just like shopping for the perfect birthday gift. Use what you learned about the prospect and send something personalized. After I met with the executive who was training for a triathlon, I sent him an article with triathlon training tips and a humorous story about something that happened to me while running.

When an executive mentioned that he would not be able to make a decision about working with me for several weeks as he was leaving on vacation, I sent him an email with several quotations about the power of taking time off with a note about fully enjoying every moment of his trip. This simple email was very well received because it was personal and authentic.

Use your creativity to find the ideal follow up ideas for each prospect. I have so much fun creating ways to follow up with my prospects in unusual and memorable ways.

The zaniest follow-up technique I've used thus far was a baby kangaroo! I was working for a facility which had a baby kangaroo trained in pet therapy. When I discovered that one of my prospects was a huge animal lover, I made arrangements to bring the kangaroo to his office. He was so excited that he invited some of his patients to come to the office that day and meet the kangaroo. I made it an event by having photos taken, framing them, and presenting them to my prospect. He became a very satisfied customer.

In a few weeks, the word got out in my community that I had a baby kangaroo, which would visit physicians' offices. Soon, prospects were inviting me to call on them. While other sales reps were delivering brochures, I was driving around town with a baby kangaroo in diapers in the front seat of my car.

Now you may not have access to a baby kangaroo, but you do have plenty of resources available for creative follow-up if you put your mind to it. I recently met with a woman who was the administrator of a healthcare organization. She mentioned that she loved to cook, and we talked about how challenging it can be to find new ways to fix chicken.

After that meeting, I called my mom and got a chicken recipe she made when I was growing up. I sent it to my prospective client and she loved it! I enjoyed adding this special touch to my follow up and cemented a solid rapport with this prospective client who later became a client.

Since you just built rapport, keep your follow up contacts light, positive and encouraging so that your prospect feels your genuine positive regard, not any pressure or manipulation.

Just for fun: If you like to cook, you can download my mom's Curry Chicken recipe here **http://rainmakermindset.com/readerbonus/**

My friend and sales colleague, Ginny Lemmerman, was selling a database product to librarians who worked in law firms. She had an interested librarian who agreed to do a one month trial of the database. However, at the end of the month, none of the attorneys in the firm had accessed the database and Ginny was concerned she would lose the sale.

Ginny got creative and found some sleeves of golf balls. She supplied them to the librarian along with a handwritten thank you note, which read:

"Ruth Smith, your librarian, would greatly appreciate your thoughts on your new environmental database.

Please accept these golf balls for yourself or a friend, in return for your feedback. I'd appreciate hearing from you by next Monday. Good luck on the tee! "

Within a week the librarian had enough feedback from her patrons that she was delighted to purchase the product.

When I was selling residential care for patients with dementia, I would take photos of residents engaged in activities like cooking, planting a garden with local children, or art and then take the framed photos to the physicians who referred the patients to our facility. This showed the physicians that they'd referred people to a positive and engaging facility as well as encouraged additional referrals.

Follow-up can be as simple as a thank you note or emailing a relevant article or as elaborate as a visit from a baby kangaroo. The key to effective follow-up is to give your prospect something that demonstrates you listened to him and discovered something that will make him smile.

Rainmakers love to make a lasting positive impression. The best way to do that is with personalized, thoughtful and creative follow-up.

Chapter 6
Listen for Needs

"It is not your customer's job to remember you. It is your obligation and responsibility to make sure they don't have the chance to forget you."

-Patricia Fripp

The rainmaker selling approach feels easy, spacious, and relaxed. Done right, you and your prospect will come to the same conclusion: that working together is a logical and beneficial way to help her reach her goals. This approach feels gracious to your prospects because you listen more than you speak.

This step in the sales process, listening for needs, is a key to closing sales and growing your profits. Imagine that you and your prospect are putting together a large puzzle. In this step, you are listening for all the pieces of that puzzle so that you can co-create a solution for your prospect.

You begin listening for needs immediately in your conversation, but purposefully ask questions to uncover needs after you have established rapport. In some cases, this step may take place in the first conversation you have, or in a longer sales process, you may spend several meetings exploring this topic.

Contrary to popular belief, sales is a dialogue, not a monologue, where you listen deeply as your prospect speaks. This can be difficult. Many new salespeople are so excited about their product or service that they neglect this step in the process and overwhelm the prospect with all sorts of information before listening to ensure there is a match between what the prospect needs and what is offered.

If you've ever been called by a telemarketer who tried to sell you on a free trip to a resort that just so happens to offer timeshares, you may have experienced this feeling. If you were not interested in a timeshare, that conversation felt annoying and you probably hung up the phone as soon as possible.

When details are provided before a need is established, you repel instead of attract customers. I recently had a woman call me about doing a joint venture with her sales program. Unfortunately for her, she went right into her pitch about her program and didn't bother to ask me anything about mine. Turns out, it's not a fit at all. She could have saved herself a lot of time by asking me some simple questions up front to find out if we would work well together.

Key Questions

Once again, preparation will help you master this step in the rainmaker sales process. I suggest that you have at least ten questions prepared for this step in the sales process. Your goal is to explore your prospect's current situation to learn if you can help. As with step 1, establishing rapport, use open-ended questions to uncover your prospect's needs.

You may not need all ten questions. This is a dance, not a rote exercise when you simply march down a list of standard questions. Prepare a group of questions before your meeting and then let your intuition guide you to select just the right ones to use.

These are some of my favorite questions for discovering needs:

- What's your vision for your _____?
- What are some of the opportunities you are exploring?
- Why is _____ so important to you?
- What have you already tried?
- What is keeping you from achieving your goal?
- How have you already invested time and money in solving this challenge?
- What are the most important things you'd like to accomplish this year?
- What outcomes do you seek?
- What is important to you about this?
- What help or resources do you need to accomplish this?
- What factors are governing your timing?

Listen deeply here. Your prospect will generally be delighted to share his ambitions, hopes, dreams, and aspirations about his vision for the future. Use as many questions as you need to develop a clear picture of your prospect and his situation.

There Are No Cookie Cutter Prospects

Remember that all people are different and have unique motivations. When I coach salespeople, it would be easy for me to assume that each of them is motivated by the same thing, but I would be wrong. For example, my client Ted is highly driven to earn as much money as possible because he loves to sail and is saving up for a boat. Julie is a mom with small children, so she is motivated to have as much free time as possible. Sue is highly competitive and thrives on recognition as a top performer in her company.

Never assume you know what a prospect really wants or why she desires it. Instead, discover this information while you are listening to the responses to your questions.

Go Even Deeper

Once you have a good understanding of where your prospect is today and where he wants to go in the future, begin to more fully explore some of his challenges. Use questions like:

- You mentioned that you really want
  _____. What seems to be getting in
  the way?
- What have you already tried?
- What is this costing you in terms of time
  and money?

Is She Lost?

If you observe that your prospect has glazed eyes, shifting body language, or seems distracted, it is important to check her level of interest in furthering the conversation. She may be overwhelmed by the stress of the situation, be deeply considering her situation, or feel ready to close the conversation. Don't assume you have made an error and she isn't interested in your offer.

Instead, ask a question. I like to check in with people periodically during the conversation to see how the process feels. Questions such as:

- How are you doing so far?
- Where are you in this process?
- Are you interested in exploring some solutions?

These check-in questions serve a dual purpose. They help your prospect to feel respected and in control of the pace of the discussion....which means you don't appear to be a pushy salesperson.

Additionally, these questions give you the opportunity to get mini yeses all the way through your discussion. You want to establish a pattern of agreement in your conversation, not so that you are brainwashing your prospect to agree with you, but to ensure that the process is agreeable and enjoyable before you move to the next steps.

Acknowledge What You Hear

At this point, your prospect may be sharing some sensitive information about her hopes, dreams, frustrations and pain. Be empathetic and acknowledge any pain that she shares with supportive comments like, "That must have been so disappointing."

However, be careful not to turn a sales meeting into a therapy session. You are listening to your prospect to establish a need for your services, not to go deeply into her past pain.

In his book, *Power Questions*, Andrew Sobel suggests using questions to focus on positive experiences rather than painful ones. In my experience, this concept is very effective at this point in a sales conversation as well. After I hear some emotionally laden information, I acknowledge it and then ask a question to shift into a more positive memory. Use questions such as:

- Tell me about your best day as a _____?
- What's your favorite day in business thus far?

This positive question helps you establish what your prospect values most. Here's an example of how this works:

Last week I was talking with a woman who was considering investing in coaching. After she expressed some of her pain and challenges, I asked her to describe her favorite day in sales. She told me a story about developing a presentation for a very large corporate account. She worked hard to create a stellar presentation and delivered it with panache to her peers in preparation of sharing it with her prospective clients. She recalled the praise and applause from her peers after her presentation and how she felt on top of the world.

When I heard this story, I remarked that selling success isn't always just about the money, that sometimes we just want to be recognized and praised.

My prospect gasped. She realized in that moment that she deeply missed feeling praised and recognized as part of a sales team. Her isolation was leading to boredom and lackluster sales results.

Once we identified her issue during this conversation, it was easy for her to see the value of coaching. In fact, she told me she needed a coach and we immediately moved forward to closing the sale.

How Urgent is This Issue?

After you have discovered the real need in your conversation, as well as the deeply held values of your prospect, assess his sense of urgency by asking questions such as:

- How important is it that you solve this issue quickly?
- Is this something that you want to pursue in the next few days, weeks, or months?

It is crucial to understand the urgency of the issue for your prospect. It may be that he does not have the time or bandwidth to address the problem now, but will do so later. For example, if a company is undergoing a re-organization it may be an ideal time for them to train their staff or it may need to wait until all the staffing changes have been made. An individual may be extremely interested in your coaching services but not able to start working with you until a family crisis is resolved. By asking your prospect to share his sense of urgency with you, you'll be able to propose a solution that seems tailor-made for him, making it feel easy and logical for him to say yes.

Choice Point

When you have reached the end of this stage of the sales process, you should know:

- What motivates your prospect
- Her vision for the future
- What her obstacles are
- How much time and money she has already invested in this issue
- How quickly she wants to solve the problem
- How you feel about the prospect
- Your level of desire to work with her

At this point in the rainmaker selling approach, you have reached a crossroads. Based on what you have gleaned during this discussion, you can either move forward to the next step in the sales process, set an appointment to meet at a later date when he is more ready to move forward, or graciously close the relationship because there is not a match between you.

If you feel there is a match between his needs and your offer, proceed directly to chapter 7 and discover what to do next.

Chapter 7
Sell to Needs and Find the Opportunity

"We each sell a little piece of happiness. You are elevating someone's spirit in some way, and to do that you have to understand the source of their angst and then you have to frame your product as a solution."

~ Sonia Marciano

At this point in your sales process, you've done lots of listening. You've uncovered your prospect's values, needs, and sense of urgency. Now it's time for you to take the lead in the conversation and suggest ways to proceed.

Remember the children's game, Red Light/Green Light?

I used to love playing that game with my friends. One person would be 'it' and line up about twenty feet away from the others. He'd turn around and call out, "Green light!" and we'd all start to run forward until we heard "Red light!" and he turned around to face us. Anyone who was still moving had to go back to the beginning. The goal of the game was to tag 'it' before he could catch you moving. The trick to this game was to move smoothly so that you can freeze instantly until you are within reach of 'it'.

In sales, the ultimate goal is to ask for the commitment or close the sale. You ask for permission to get to the next yes and to move the sales process forward. If you get an objection, a red light, you stop and ask more questions until you get the next green light, or yes, then you proceed.

It is an art and a science to know when and how to smoothly move into the next step in the sales process. This step can be difficult for people new to sales. It is sometimes challenging to shift from the discovery phase into asking for a sale.

For example, my client Brenda, a medical sales representative, often became such good friends with the doctors she called on that she never asked for any sales or referrals. She'd convinced herself that if one of her doctors wanted to buy, he'd ask her when he was ready. She loved establishing rapport and listening for needs but avoided asking for a sale. No wonder her sales were down.

Top performing salespeople ask for the sale every time they hear a buying signal. This step can be uncomfortable if you don't put a process in place. Be cognizant of asking for mini yeses. You may feel pressured to ask for the sale prematurely because you are dreading hearing no or you may procrastinate and let the conversation disintegrate into a nice chat instead of a sales call. Let me show you how to make this easier.

Listen for Buying Signals

During the course of your conversation, you'll start to hear a rising excitement in prospects who are ready to move forward. The cadence and tone of their voice will change. They may start to speak more quickly or more hopefully about the future. New ideas may be popping up as you help them see what's possible.

These subtle changes are called buying signs. It's critical to be able to identify the buying signs so that you know exactly when to ask your prospect to become your client.

If you fail to recognize buying signs, you run the risk of overselling your services and missing the window of opportunity when a prospect is most receptive to becoming one of your clients. If you continue to share information or deliver your presentation to a prospect that has already communicated buying signals, that prospect can interpret this as inattention on your part. Either way, an inability to pick up on your prospect's signals may cost you a client.

When you hear a buying sign, you know that your prospect is ready to discuss how she can take ownership of your product or services and how it would specifically benefit and work for her. In other words, she is now sold on your service and is ready to discuss purchasing from you.

Buying signals are usually statements or questions from the prospect; these inquiries bring them one step closer to the comfort zone of making the purchase. You've asked him a series of questions and piqued his interest. In turn, he is now asking you or telling you how and when he likes to buy.

Buying signs can show up within the first few minutes of a conversation, or they may not emerge until the end of your meeting. They can show up at any time. It's up to you to pay attention to these signals, so that you can adjust your conversation accordingly and approach the close when it's most appropriate to do so.

When a prospect is ready to buy, he will start to ask you questions. Listen for questions like these which signal a prospect's interest to learn more or to buy:

- What's your process like?
- How quickly can we get started?
- How long would we work together?
- How much money do you need to begin this service?
- Do you offer financing?
- Have you worked with other individuals/ companies in my area?
- Can I speak to one of your current customers?
- Do you offer a guarantee?
- What are the outcomes/results I will receive if we work together?
- Can I do this in stages?
- How have others benefited from using your product or service?

Don't Fear Questions

Many new salespeople are put off by questions or objections. They believe that questions and objections express doubt about the offer. However, in my experience, questions are to be celebrated! When a prospect is interested enough to ask questions, he is signaling his interest and willingness to learn more about your product or service.

Often people with the most questions are those who make decisions slowly after gathering all the facts. By providing a spacious conversation in which to address those questions, you are increasing the trust your prospect feels towards you and demonstrating that you care enough to create an individualized solution for her need.

Questions also give you the opportunity to demonstrate how your product or service is different from your competitors. You don't need to trash anyone else, but you can clearly show how what you have to offer measures up against other products or services and explain how your offer would be best suited to help your prospect meet her goals.

Manage Your Mindset

This stage in the sales process requires a positive mindset and belief that you can serve the person in front of you in some way. Assume that you will help your prospect meet his needs successfully. When you approach the needs conversation with that mindset, your goal is to create a solution and to be a resource for your prospect. This feels very different from trying to convince someone to buy.

Top performing salespeople are resourceful. As you continue to explore your prospect's needs and answer her questions, focus on serving her and helping her reach her goals. If you genuinely cannot serve your prospect, refer her to another company which may be a better fit. This generous action may lead to wonderful referrals for you in the future.

A Deeper Meaning in Some Buying Signals

When you hear lots of questions about your past experience or your process, it could very well be that your prospect has had negative experiences with other salespeople or products in the past. This prospect may be skeptical and looking for the reassurance and support that she is making the right decision with you.

Often prospective clients repeat the same question several times. He may simply want to hear an answer more than once to see if you provide a consistent answer or he hasn't fully understood all of the information and wants to hear it again.

These assurance seeking questions may sound like:

- Do you think this will solve my problem?
- Can you tell me about your pricing packages again?

- Will you go over those payment terms once more?
- How quickly will I see a return on my investment?

How to Respond to Buying Signals

When I hear buying signals, I'll summarize the conversation thus far and then ask permission to share a story. Use language like this, "It seems like you have a very important goal to grow your business, so that you can leave your day job. I'm not sure if it would be a fit or not, but would you like to hear a story about one of my other coaching clients who had a similar goal? Would that be of interest to you?"

Short, memorable stories make your offer tangible to your prospects and aid in the decision making process. When you share a success story, your prospect can imagine what it would be like to work with you and achieve similar results.

It's wise to have a few stories prepared so that you can easily insert them into a sales conversation when you hear a buying signal. Include this information in each of the stories:

- What was your client's big vision?
- What problem or challenge was your client trying to solve?
- Why was your experience or expertise important?
- Why did your client select you or your product over a competitor? What differentiated you for this client?

- What was the one memorable value the customer received from your product or service? Just use one here.

When you share a sales story, you are demonstrating that what you have to offer will be of value to your prospect.

After you've shared a sales story, ask for permission to share some of the features and benefits of what you have to offer. Remember to stress the benefits more than the features. Your prospect may not care that your program meets on Thursday afternoons, but she will care if she can learn how to solve a pressing problem by participating in that program.

A smooth way to enter this segment of the conversation is to ask, "Tell me, what you would like to know about this?"

This question allows your prospect to guide the conversation to the information that is the most important to her.

Include the emotional benefits as well as the practical ones. People buy emotionally, even when they believe they are logical decision makers. Remind them how great it will feel to be supported, to have an edge over their competition, or to help more people. Use the values that you uncovered in your previous conversations.

Continue to check in with your prospect and see how he is feeling about the information you are presenting. Ask open-ended questions such as

How would this support you in reaching your goal of _____?"

Continue to address his needs and soon you will be ready to close the sale. Turn the page and learn how rainmakers make a sale.

Chapter 8
Close and Keep the Sale

"Some people fold after making one timid request. They quit too soon. Keep asking until you find the answers. In sales there are usually four or five "nos" before you get a "yes."

~Jack Canfield

During my first week selling books door-to-door for the Southwestern Company, I was a mess. I kept forgetting my sales process whenever I sat down in a home with a prospective buyer. The only thing I could remember to do was show people the books I had with me. I spent a long time leafing through the books, ignoring the glazed eyes and impatient body language of my prospects.

Many new salespeople have the same challenge. They have solid knowledge of the product or service they are offering. By default, they spend a long time discussing feature and benefits and are then frustrated when no one buys.

Let me share my proven rainmaker tips for closing the sale. Once you implement this information, you will see a great increase in the number of sales you close and feel so much more confident about your ability to generate sales for your business.

Closing the sale is step 5 in the rainmaker selling system. However, you are actually using the closing process in each step of the sales process each time you ask for small commitments to move forward. Prior to beginning your close, you have:

Step 1 - Filled your pipeline, organized your contact list and prioritized who to call on and follow up with...

Step 2 - Established rapport, asked your clients about their vision and their story, and often shared your own story for them to get to know you better and to show your own vulnerability, made a connection. Asked for commitment for next step.

Step 3 - Listened for needs and opportunities, then asked more questions which leads to the next step.

Step 4 - Sold to meet those needs by clarifying, finding solutions together, and shared others' success stories.

Now you are ready to close and keep the sale. This final part of the process will feel like a logical next step if you have completed the other steps successfully and what you offer is a good match for your prospect.

Listen for Closing Signals

Your prospect will tell you when he is ready to move into the close. He will start to ask specific questions such as:

- When does your program begin?
- Can you give me some references from previous customers?
- What is included in your package?
- Do you offer any bonuses?
- Do you have an application process?
- What are your fees, what's the cost?

A prospect may come up with additional objections at this point, which some sellers think they need to hit, bombard, or squelch. That approach is not effective, in fact, in my experience, quite the opposite is true.

I was speaking with a salesperson named Jeff recently who had made a career change from direct selling to sales coaching. Jeff was not happy with his career move. I asked him more about his coaching experience. He told me he was frustrated with salespeople who didn't take his direct advice. Jeff told me about one sales rep who didn't understand how to deal with customer objections. Jeff told the rep you need to hit back hard when the customer objects and tell them why they're wrong.

Unfortunately, Jeff's approach is not successful. Arguing or making a prospect feel wrong will repel him and make him run for the hills. When a customer/client raises an objection, it's a great opportunity for you to identify what's really on his mind. You should acknowledge the objection, don't gloss over it or tell him why he's wrong.

Then open up a discussion around the objection, ask more questions, and then invite him to share more about his ideas surrounding the objection to see if you can both create a solution. This is a wonderful opportunity to make a powerful connection, and perhaps to share a story of someone who had the same objection and how your services or product helped them.

Don't Rush to the Close

When you hear a closing signal, resist the temptation to rush your client to sign on the bottom line immediately. Remember that the rainmaker selling system is client centered and gracious so this is not the time to put pressure on your prospect.

However, your prospect does depend on you to lead her through the closing process. If you have been hearing mini yeses through the course of your prior discussion, followed by some closing signals, assume you have a match and lead your prospect through the process of becoming your client with confidence.

You will do this by answering all questions thoroughly and continuing to ask questions to ensure your prospect is still with you. Use questions like:

- What do you like so far?
- Is this making sense?
- What's not clear at this point?
- How is this landing for you?
- How does this align with your goals?
- What do you think?
- How could I make doing business with me easier?
- How can you see me supporting you in achieving your goals?
- How can I be of the greatest help to you in our relationship?
- What questions can I help you answer?

Of course, you will not use all these questions. Use this list and your intuition to select the questions which will be useful to the prospect in front of you. Because you have been listening closely during all of your interactions with this prospect, you'll be able to choose questions that will allow your prospect to consider your offer carefully and then decide if it feels right.

Using questions at this point is much more effective than trying to hammer your prospect into a yes by talking about the features and benefits of your offer. These questions will help your prospect feel safe during the closing process because you are providing all the information she needs and ensuring that she feels supported during the process. They will also help you avoid overwhelming your prospect with extraneous information that is not important to her.

The Prospect Sets the Pace

Remember that people buy differently. Some will want all the facts and details, others want to move rapidly and begin right away.

For example, I spoke with a woman a few weeks ago who came to our initial call with a list of questions. She was not forthcoming with much personal information and seemed reluctant to chat very much. Instead, she asked very detailed questions about my work and my background.

Finally she said, "I have a deadline. I need structure. How do I apply for your program?"

By listening closely, I learned that she wanted to lead the conversation, had done thorough research already, and wanted to quickly close the sale and get the help she needed.

Other prospects require several discussions and a long period of time before they are ready to say yes. Your goal as a rainmaker is to determine the buying style of each of your prospects and adapt your pace to match.

When you do this, you will automatically increase your sales. Every prospect is unique. When you customize your approach and your pace after listening for buying signals, you will hear yes much more often.

Coping with No

I was speaking with a prospect recently regarding an upcoming coaching program. The conversation was going very well until he revealed that he was not interested in a program. Rather than become defensive, I asked him to tell me more. He shared he'd had a poor experience in other group programs and felt his needs were not addressed adequately.

This information was a great closing signal for me. I could tell that he wanted individual attention, a solid return on his investment, and a personalized experience.

I explained how my program was structured differently than many similar programs and that it included some one-on-one coaching sessions with me. I also mentioned that I offered a private option where he could work through the same curriculum with me personally at a higher price point.

Once he reviewed the differences between my program and the others he'd participated in, as well as the options available to him, he chose the group program.

When you hear a no, explore it with your prospect to understand the roadblock. It may be a negative past experience or that the prospect does not really see the value in your offer. Probe to find out what else he needs. Again, ask if it's okay to share a story about a former client who had similar concerns. You can also suggest he speak with a satisfied client.

Zig Ziglar, one of my favorite authors, motivational speakers and salesman, always talked about the "5 Sales Objections":

- No Need
- No Money
- No Hurry
- No Desire
- No Trust

With all due respect to Zig, I like to refer to these concepts as the 5 Sales Opportunities. When I hear a no, I begin to explore these areas with my prospect to determine which opportunities are present and which ones are lacking.

For each prospect, during my conversations, I am trying to:

- Find the Need
- Find the Money
- Find the Urgency
- Find the Desire
- Find the Trust

When I hear a no, I may refer back to our earlier conversations and discuss urgency, need, or desire. Here are some sample questions for each of those areas:

- Urgency: "You know, Jim, you mentioned earlier that you were concerned about meeting your quarterly goals and the end of the quarter is coming up pretty soon. Do you think that working with me would help you reach that goal?"

- Need: "Marie, you were telling me a while ago that you need to increase your revenues by 25%. How do you think this program could help you increase your sales?"

- Need: "John, I remember in our very first conversation, you were telling me 'we have a sales problem. It's two-fold - part of it is our messaging and the other part is that we lack an efficient sales process.' Tell me how implementing a better message and a succinct sales process would get your sales team on the right track to boost sales?"

- Desire: "Dr. Hansen, you were telling me how much you wanted to see faster recovery times for your patients after surgery. If this device could speed up the healing process for your patients, would that be helpful?"

If you really believe in your product or service and that your prospect could benefit from it, explore those initial 'nos' and see if you can find a way to transform them into a yes.

Fear in Disguise

When a prospect declines your offer, you may hear these two common reasons:

- I can't afford this.
- I don't have time.

These reasons are fears in disguise. They signal that your prospect does not see the value in your offer. Your response is to ask questions to explore those fears and shift them if possible.

It is wise to validate your prospect's concerns about lack of money and lack of time. In today's economy and fast-paced environment, money and time may be precious commodities. However, your prospect has already shared her vision for the future, why it is important to her, and her commitment to reaching that goal. Probe gently and curiously to discover why your prospect tells you she wants to reach a goal and yet feels uncomfortable investing time and resources to make that goal a reality.

Your tone of voice is very important here. Don't interrogate your prospect or make her feel defensive, just gently inquire.

Try asking, "You know, Theresa, I'm a little confused here. Earlier you were so passionate about growing your business. Your voice was so full of energy and excitement. Now you seem reluctant to invest in making your goal a reality. Can you tell me what you are thinking right now?"

When your prospect answers this question, you'll know how to proceed. If she states that she is just not interested in your offer now, you can graciously close the conversation by thanking her for her time and asking if she knows anyone else who might be a good fit for your work. Instead, if she shares a concern or belief that she will not benefit from your offer, you can explore that with her and provide more information or more options.

How to Discuss Price

When you are selling professional services or a tangible product, it can be challenging to know how to discuss the cost, especially if you are new to sales. It is wise not to use words like cost, price, tuition, or fees during discussions with your prospect. Instead, use the word investment.

You are offering support in reaching a cherished goal and a valued dream. Encourage your prospect to view your offer as an investment in his future. I recently heard an interview with Warren Buffet and Anthony Robbins in which they stressed that success comes from continually seeing the value of investing in themselves in order to reach their goals. You are asking your prospect to make an investment in her future success so talking about the long-range benefits and return on investment is important when you are discussing the funds required for that investment.

Remember we talked about clearly articulating the value of your offer?

When I sold books, I was really offering education for families. When I sold medical devices, I was offering physicians tools to heal their patients. Today, when I sell coaching and consulting services, I am really offering a sales system that brings a dependable, consistent stream of income into a business. That could be termed business security, business success, or profitability.

As you discuss the investment your prospect will make in your product or service, be sure to tie it back to the ultimate value you provide.

If you sell a very high-end product or service which could be perceived as expensive by your prospect, be ready to share why the service is a great value. My fellow sales trainer Colleen Stanley has an excellent way of discussing high-end services. She says "Many of our clients purchased on price before working with us. They would find what they needed at the lowest possible price and have to make do with services that were not quite a good fit or hassle with poor customer service. We pride ourselves in both great customer service and tailor-made solutions so when you join us, you can be certain of a great experience."

How can you create a similar statement that educates your prospect on the tangible and intangible value she will receive from your offer?

Be a Bold Rainmaker

After fully exploring your prospects' fears and opportunities, it's time to take a risk and just ask for the business. You've already invested time and energy in exploring your prospect's challenges, vision, and goals. When the energy is high, a rainmaker will simply ask for the business.

I like to use questions here as well because you've already established a pattern of questions and answers in the conversation so continuing this pattern won't feel pushy to your prospect.

These sample questions give you an idea of how to ask for the business:

- Are you ready to move forward?
- What is the next action for you in the decision making process?

- Have we discussed everything you need to make your decision?
- Can we initiate the paperwork today?
- Or if you want to keep it light and fun you can say… "Let's get this party started!"

Rainmakers don't wait for prospects to tell them they are ready to buy. That may happen occasionally, but for the most part, your prospects need you to ask them to buy. Do this boldly and with confidence because you've already established a great fit between your offer and her needs.

Here's how it might sound when you are sure of a perfect fit between the prospect and your offer:

"You know, Sally, everything we've talked about today tells me that coaching is a perfect fit for you and will help you reach your goal of bringing in 10 new clients in the next 90 days. How will you feel when you've met that goal?"

Sally replies with something about feeling proud.

"Ok, if you want to feel that sense of pride and accomplishment, let me help you get there. When shall we schedule our first coaching session?"

I like to say that rainmakers are pleasantly persistent. When you get just as excited for the future of your prospect as she is, it's natural to invite her to take advantages of the resources you offer. It's fun for both of you to say yes to working together.

Options and Discounts

People buy emotionally but want to have logical reasons that will help them justify the purchase in their minds. Providing options and choices can help you nudge a prospect off the fence and towards making a decision.

I will often offer a quick decision bonus for prospective clients who say yes in a specific time period. Rather than discounting my services, which implies that they are overpriced, I'll add in a bonus, which signals generosity.

The conversation may be on the phone or via email. It might sound like this:

"David, I really enjoyed speaking with you today. It sounds like you are ready to go and that my program could be the answer for you. What I'd like to do is put a special offer out there for you. If you're really excited about getting your business up and running and you want to enroll by Saturday, 30th of June for our July 10th program, I will offer two extra individual coaching sessions prior to the start of our program so you can build momentum coming into the program and are that much more prepared. That will put you ahead of the game. I'm offering this to the next three coaches coming into the program. Would you be interested in this extra bonus?"

Many times, prospects want to say yes and are looking for a little nudge to help them make a decision. You can offer that nudge with a fast action bonus offer. If you don't want to offer a bonus, you can invite your prospect to select from a couple of options.

Your conversation may sound like this: "Linda, it sounds like my ride-along coaching program is a perfect fit for you. I would love to go with you on your sales calls and mentor you so that you can increase your sales numbers. There are two ways you can get started. You can complete the application form online with me now so that I can walk you through it, or I can email you the link and you can fill it out on your own. Which would be best for you?"

Be careful here not to overwhelm your prospect with too many options or too much talking. If he has given you clear buying signals you don't have to keep on selling, just ask for the business, give two or three options, and stay silent. Let your prospect decide what's best, assuming he wants to move forward.

Keeping the Sale After It's Made

Have you ever purchased an expensive piece of clothing? If so, the clerk probably complimented you on it as you were checking out saying something like "Oh, that color really brings out your eyes." That clerk's been trained to help you love that great suit you just purchased so you are not tempted to return it.

Rainmakers know that a little additional follow up will cement a sale and prevent any buyer's remorse. Once your prospect has agreed to your offer, continue to follow up and ensure that she feels great about her purchase. Send a thank you note, provide any bonus items, and ensure a smooth delivery of the product or service. You can also assign some initial field work to encourage him to use your material immediately.

Treat your new client like a treasured family member. This will lead to a happy client who may purchase from you repeatedly.

Don't forget to ask for referrals. Now that your new client has experienced the pleasure of buying from you and knows that you deliver on your promises, she is the ideal person to open doors for you. Rainmakers always ask for referrals.

Some may think this is too soon to gain referral business, I see it as an opportune time. It is when your clients and customers are excited to work with you and want to pass on that enthusiasm to their colleagues or bring a friend along to experience coaching or the product or services you provide.

When I worked in medical sales I made it a point to ask for referrals from physicians as soon as they started giving me business. I printed out a form and put it on a clipboard, and when they had a patient to refer, they could write it on the handy form. Whenever they glanced at that clipboard, it was a reminder to them to contact me immediately.

When I'm asking for referrals in my coaching business, I will ask for a strong testimonial from a client to share with a prospective coaching client.

I often ask coaching clients to refer me to other companies they know of or do business with. If the client moves to a new company, I ask them to put me in contact with the decision makers there to open up a dialogue around coaching.

I don't wait until I'm done with my coaching sessions to ask for referrals. I believe the best time to ask is when someone has just hired you as they are enthusiastic and often want others to have the same experience and success they are embarking on. My mantra is ASK: people have every right to say no but usually they are happy to support me in growing my business.

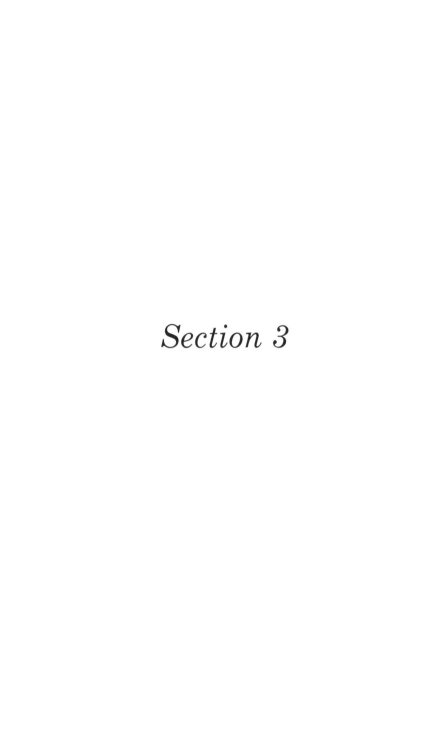

Section 3

Sales is a great profession. It affords flexibility, fun, constant challenge, and the opportunity to meet great new people every day.

When you become a rainmaker, whether you are selling your own products or services, or you are selling for another, you have a set of skills, which many lack. These skills can increase your income, give you more free time, and provide security.

A few months ago I started a new project with a business partner. In the next ten days I generated more than $25,000 in sales for that project, all because I had a specific sales process in place, along with a passion to help my potential clients. I also had a timetable and accountability to meet that timeline.

I set a goal, hunkered down in my office, and kept working until I'd reached that goal. I made it a game. I asked myself:

- How many qualified contacts from my warm and cool list can I reach by phone today?
- How many will respond after the first phone call?
- How many will respond after a phone call and an email?
- What is their response and how can I support them?

I split my day into three goal periods, which is something I learned from selling books door-to-door back in college. In the first goal period I made outbound calls. Goal period two was spent sending out emails. And in the third goal period, I focused on creative follow up for each contact.

It was fun and although I had a system in place, it didn't get stale because I could switch gears throughout the day and be productive in each goal period. My plan worked because I got into immediate action. This action built momentum which fueled enthusiasm and passion for helping my potential clients, and I closed more business than I originally anticipated.

Maria Church, a colleague of mine as well as an author and coach, splits her workweek into "theme days." On specific days she schedules in her writing, sales/marketing, business, education and personal tasks. This gives her a structure she can follow and helps her accomplish many tasks.

Find a system which suits your individual style and helps you reach your goals. Each time you set and reach a sales goal, you will increase your confidence and belief that you can make it rain money anytime you want.

That's the rainmaker mindset in action, and a very powerful place to be.

Is it possible for you to develop that confidence and assurance that rainmakers enjoy?

You bet! Success leads to more success. Put a process in place that makes sense to you and that you can be accountable to, follow through and make it a game. You'll be making it rain before you know it.

Chapter 9
Managing Your Time and Energy for Peak Performance

"Mental will is a muscle that needs exercise, just like the muscles of the body."

~Lynn Jennings

As you may have already discovered, the most important component of the rainmaker sales process is you. Your ability to listen deeply, communicate effectively, and think creatively will lead to more sales and more success.

You don't have to be anyone else or change your personality to be a rainmaker. Because rainmakers are authentic, you get to show up as you. And, you will make more sales when you are your very best you.

The rainmaker sales process requires the ability to transfer your positive energy to your prospects. To accomplish this, you have to possess positive energy in the first place.

Maintaining your physical and mental health is vitally important. That means eating well, exercising, and looking your best. Strong self-care increases your confidence.

Try an experiment. Go to a store or restaurant in your sloppiest clothes, don't comb your hair or apply make-up, and observe how people respond to you. Then, go back another day looking your best.

You'll notice the difference right away. You'll be perceived more professionally, treated with more courtesy, and carry yourself with more confidence.

When You Don't Invest in Self-Care

I was working with a client recently who was exhausted. He was so exhausted and stressed that he was relieved when a gatekeeper turned him away or he heard a no. He wasn't selling; he was just going through the motions and checking items off of his to-do list.

Many new coaches get into the same predicament. They are so busy setting up their websites, attending networking meetings, and completing all the small tasks a professional practice requires that they are too tired to sell well.

Rainmakers Use Routines

I have a regular routine of self-care and exercise. I realized a long time ago that while it did not matter if I was working for myself or for a large corporation, I was responsible for keeping myself in prime condition physically, mentally, and emotionally if I wanted to succeed. Creating routines and scheduling time for self-care helps me ensure that I stay balanced and enthusiastic about my work and my life.

For me, running daily and spending time at the gym is essential. I love the positive energy there and feel my best when I get regular exercise. If you don't enjoy the gym, try running, walking, dancing or yoga. Exercise will decrease your stress and increase your confidence. I often come up with my most creative ideas while running or exercising at the gym. It gets my blood flowing and creates an endorphin rush, which fills me with great ideas I can follow up with when I'm back in my office or on the phone with a client.

Feed your mind by reading. You can learn so much from books on sales, personal development, and business principles. The information you learn while you read will provide you with great conversation starters as well as practical information you can use to increase your performance.

Finally, feed your heart by spending time with loved ones, enjoying nature, listening to music or engaging in a spiritual practice that nurtures you. I firmly believe that I work with the best clients on earth and I celebrate that fact daily. I'm grateful that I work in sales where I have freedom to climb as high as I wish and earn a wonderful living. When you are happy, you'll have more positive energy to attract and engage with your clients and prospects.

Control Your Calendar So It Does Not Control You

My recommendation is that you carefully manage your calendar by grouping similar tasks together. For example, if you need to make cold calls, schedule a block of time and see how many you can do before you take a break. I like to make a game of it. I'll say, "OK Carolyn, make seven calls and then you can take a break." When I'm making warm calls and offering a specific service or product, I'll challenge myself to make a certain number of sales in a two hour block.

Making sales leads to momentum. When you start to hear a few yeses in a row, you are having a great day. Keep going! I like to challenge myself to see how long I can maintain the momentum. Like riding a wave, when you are making sales, don't stop. I had a client who wrote the word GO on a post it note on her desk and when she had doubts about getting out in front of potential clients – she would look at the word GO and it would move her into action.

Back in my book selling days, we would call the period between five and nine pm the gravy period. That was the very best time of day to make book sales. I'd sit down about 4:30 and review all the homes I'd called on earlier that day, making a priority list of the families who had children or those who asked me to return later in the day. Because I was walking or riding my bike, I'd group them so that I could visit the most homes in the shortest amount of time.

As you implement the rainmaker skills you are learning in this Quick Guide, pay attention and discover your gravy period. When are your prospects more likely to talk with you and to buy?

Through this exercise one of my clients realized that her best calling time was six to nine am. Her prospects were in three different time zones and she was most productive in making the bulk of her calls in this time period and started booking more appointments by shifting her schedule.

When you ascertain that gravy period, block it off on your calendar and don't use it for anything other than making sales, either in person or by phone. Your gravy period is your very best time to make sales so it only makes sense to reserve it solely for that purpose.

Then, use the remaining time on your calendar for creative follow-up, priming the pump by meeting additional prospects, and to take care of any record keeping.

Play the Numbers Game

Numbers are a rainmaker's best friend. If you are selling for a company, you'll probably be asked to compile sales reports for your employer. However, if you are a solo professional, selling your own products or services, you may not know what to measure.

I've created a Rainmaker Metrics Sheet, which will help you track and measure your success over time. You can download it here **http://rainmakermindset.com/readerbonus/**

Measuring your sales success is fun! It allows you to see where you have successes and where you can make improvements.

Plus, it will help you on those days when you are hearing a string of nos. There will be times when you just aren't making many sales. On those days, review your metrics. Observe:

- How are my monthly sales compared to last month?
- Have I completed fewer follow-ups?
- Is there a change in the amount of new prospects I've added to my pipeline?
- How many prospects can I speak with next week?

Purposeful Abundance

When I have plenty of prospects to call on or meet with in person, it takes the pressure off of me to sell. I am more in tune with my prospect's true needs and spend my energy uncovering whether we are a fit to serve them. If I have that feeling of abundance, I am not bothered by the nos or the ones who aren't moving forward yet. I know that when I speak and meet with enough qualified prospects, I will hit my numbers and meet my goals – often exceed them.

If you feel stressed because you don't have enough prospects in your pipeline, concentrate on filling it up. When you have plenty of people in your pipeline, you can weather a slow sales period without worry as you have many other prospects with whom you can connect.

Maintain Your Positive Outlook

Rainmakers are positive, resilient, and enjoy the sales process. Remember, you get to decide how much fun you have in life, so make your sales process fun for yourself and for your prospects.

Keep things light. Use your sense of humor and focus on the positives.

Celebrate each win, big or small.

When you bring more positive energy and fun into your sales process, you will wake up energized and excited every morning, like I do. I can't wait to meet more great people every day and find out how I can help them.

Make that your mantra and you'll be a rainmaker too.

Chapter 10
The Next Steps on Your Rainmaker Journey

"I know that I have the ability to achieve the object of my Definite Purpose in life, therefore, I demand of myself persistent, continuous action toward its attainment, and I here and now promise to render such action."

~ Napoleon Hill

Congratulations! You've reached the end of this quick guide and now understand the rainmaker sales process, mindset, and advanced communication skills required to consistently and joyfully make sales. You are ready to make it rain!

Now it is time for you to implement what you've learned. You can read all the books on sales you like, but without implementation, your results won't change.

To make implementing the rainmaker sales approach as easy as possible, consider hiring a coach or mentor for accountability and to help you set goals, brainstorm, and stay committed to your progress. I meet with my coach weekly and find it to be the most important thirty minutes of my week. To be a high performer in sales, or in any other endeavor, you need a coach. I also belong to a mastermind group of female sales experts. We are a global group and meet monthly on Skype where we share sales ideas and support each other with goals to continually make us stretch and challenge ourselves. Accountability is key to our success.

It is also important that you surround yourself with positive role models. Identify rainmaker sales professionals in your industry and in your community and spend time with them. Share ideas, network, and support each other. Great sales techniques are effective in any industry so the more rainmakers you network with, the more you will learn.

While you are implementing, I suggest that you create two sets of monthly goals, 'achievable goals' and 'dream goals.' Write them down where you can see them daily. Then visualize yourself reaching those dream goals. You'll be surprised at how often you are able to come close to or even exceed your dream goals with consistent effort.

It is also very helpful to document your progress and your achievements. When self-doubt creeps in, I pull out my resume and review my career accomplishments. I recall my successes and find my confidence streaming back in.

Remember the line from Alan Weiss, "The first sale is to yourself." **If you don't wake up feeling this way**, your job number one is to "sell yourself" on what you have (or your company has) to offer the world—that you have something of such great value that you would be remiss if you didn't offer to others. **When you really believe that to the core of your being**, it's amazing how your energy will shift.

Try writing a check to yourself for the income you want to make monthly and yearly. Put that check where you can see it each morning and use to as a motivator for continued action and achievement.

Next create a written document, which supports you in achieving that dollar amount. Work backwards and write a plan that keeps you accountable daily, weekly and monthly to reach that annual income. If your goal is an idea in thin air, it's just a dream. If it's written down, it becomes crystallized and attainable.

When you implement these action steps and the rainmaker sales process, you'll be astounded at how much more enjoyment you feel when selling and how many more sales you can make.

Remember the sales cycle assessment you completed in the first section of the book? I challenge you to re-evaluate your skill level every month until you have mastered all the steps in the rainmaker selling process.

Commit to taking at least three actions each month to strengthen the areas of the sales cycle where you have opportunities for improvement.

You can download additional copies of the assessment at **http://rainmakermindset.com/ readerbonus/**

This rainmaker process works....and it will work for you. I urge you to begin today and start reaping the personal and business benefits you so richly deserve!

About the Author

 Carolyn is a Professional Certified Coach (PCC, CPC) by International Coach Academy (ICA), and accredited through International Coach Federation (ICF). Today her global coaching clients benefit from the skills she learned and applied successfully during her 30 year sales and management career. She coaches groups, one-to-one clients, and delivers group workshops and public speaking.

Carolyn understands the value of the rainmaker mindset. She began her sales career as a college sophomore selling educational books door-to-door for the Southwestern Company. After college, she became a top sales professional in a variety of industries.

In 1994, Carolyn chose a career in medical sales, where she quickly rose to the top 1% of producers and remained there, until 2009, when she started her own sales coaching, consulting and training company, Rainmaker Mindset, LLC. She coaches VP's of Sales and Sales Managers to build high performance sales teams. She has a proven selling strategy that helps sales professionals get in with the gatekeepers, fill their pipelines with new prospects, meet with the decision makers and boost sales.

Carolyn has traveled around the globe for business and pleasure. An avid athlete and youth track coach, Carolyn has completed seven marathons including the prestigious Boston Marathon, and numerous other races. Carolyn lives in Southern California with her husband, Andy, two sons, Cole and Cooper, and their Great Dane, Lilly Kate.

Acknowledgements

So many people have contributed to my success and to the writing of this book. I am filled with gratitude for:

My husband Andy – the best sounding board alive, who supports me daily with my sales endeavors and is always happy to proofread my blogs and book chapters.

My two boys, Cole and Cooper, who are always there to receive and offer unconditional love, no matter what kind of a day I've had.

Ginny & Darrell Lemmerman, and Dave Causer, my first sales managers with the Southwestern Company, who recruited, trained and coached me on how to implement the cycle of a sale and excel at my craft.

Monica Llano, one of my Medical Sales Managers, for giving me the book "How to Become a Rainmaker" by Jeffrey J. Fox.

David Christopher and Randy Murphy for hiring me at RS Medical.

Connie Putnam, my high school cross country running coach, for teaching me that "the hills are my friends". He came to watch me run the Boston Marathon 15 years after I graduated from high school and we're still in contact today.

Bronwyn Bowery-Ireland and Karen Cappello, my coaches at The International Coach Academy (ICA), where I received top notch coach training and tremendous support to embark on my own coaching practices.

Jill Konrath for inviting me to her annual Sales Shebang for women sales experts.

My Sales Shebang mastermind group, where we encourage each other and hold each other accountable to excelling at our craft.

I'd also like to thank my fellow sales trainers and coaches who contributed stories to this book. Appreciation and thanks to Janice Mars, Colleen Stanley, Jill Konrath, Julie Hansen, Alice Kemper, Lori Richardson, Babette Ten Haken, and Ginny Lemmerman.

To my competitors I've met on my 30-year sales journey of selling books, actors, medical devices and services and sales coaching. You've all made me aspire to be my best and reach higher.

I also want to thank the prospects who told me no. You spurred me on to find the next yes and taught me persistence and resilience.

Special thanks to my clients. I've learned from each of you and feel inspired to work with you every day.

Lynne Klippel, my editor in chief, and her team at Thomas Noble Books who brought this book to life.

Special thanks to Jennifer Kinsman and Monica Chizzo for swooping in like angels at just the right moment. You are the best.

Resources

These helpful resources will assist you in becoming a Rainmaker.

Rainmaker Mindset www.rainmakermindset.com

Books

Almost every top performing salesperson I know is a voracious reader. Here's a list of some of my favorite authors and their books about selling:

Malcolm Gladwell - *Outliers*

Jill Konrath - *Snap Selling* and *Selling to Big Companies*

Brian Tracy - *Eat That Frog*

Andrew Sobel and Jerald Panas - *Power Questions*

Andy Paul Zero - *Time Selling*

Jeffery J. Fox - *How to Become A Rainmaker*

Napoleon Hill - *Think and Grow Rich*

Marcus Buckingham -*The Truth About You*

Julie Hansen - *ACT Like a Sales Pro*

Bernadette McClelland - *The First Sale is Always to Yourself*

Babette Ten Haken - *Do YOU Mean Business?*

Colleen Stanley - *Emotional Intelligence for Sales Success*

Zig Ziglar - *Secrets of Closing the Sale*

Are You Ready for More Support?

Did this quick guide make you hungry for more support and more sales?

My Rainmaker Mindset Sales Coaching and Training might be a perfect fit to help you improve your mindset and add more profit to your bottom line.

Please visit http://rainmakermindset.com to access additional information on my blog as well to learn more about all the ways I can help you become a Rainmaker.

Made in the USA
Charleston, SC
26 August 2013